QUIRKY
LEADERSHIP

QUIRKY
LEADERSHIP

PERMISSION
GRANTED

JOHN VOELZ

Abingdon Press™

Nashville

Quirky Leadership

Permission Granted

Copyright © 2013 by John Voelz

All rights reserved.

This book is printed on acid-free paper.

Library of Congress Cataloging-in-Publication Data on file

ISBN 978-1-4267-5491-3

13 14 15 16 17 18 19 20 21—10 9 8 7 6 5 4 3 2 1

MANUFACTURED IN THE UNITED STATES OF AMERICA

CONTENTS

This book is dedicated to the staff of Westwinds Church. You are some of the quirkiest people I know.

SHOUT OUTS

TAHNI

Tahni (my wife)—Thanks for letting me write on my days off. And weekends. And evenings. A lot of what I've learned about being a leader I have learned by watching you successfully run a business the last twenty years. You have softened me as a leader, which I'm sure is a frightening thought to some who may wonder how I *used* to operate.

DAVID McDONALD

David McDonald—No book could contain the horde of inside jokes (You don't understand!) that tell the story of our shared conquests and malfunctions. If we were superheroes, we'd be the Wonder Twins. You'd be the girl one.

BRAD FRANKLIN

Brad Franklin—Thanks for being my friend for more than twenty-five years. I've grown so much as a leader in the church by watching you, disagreeing well with you, praying with you, chatting with you, taking risks with you, following your lead, and watching you bleed for the church. Thanks for always celebrating my quirkiness without surrendering yours.

PREFACE

Beginning almost nine years ago, three men landed at West-winds Community Church in Jackson, Michigan, within months of each other. I was the first to arrive. My family and I moved out from California to take advantage of a timely window of opportunity to do something daring and different. My friend, Randy Shafer, came a couple of months after me by way of Peoria, Illinois.

Picture me during this time as a cockeyed optimist—a bright, young artist with dreams to change the world and do something with lasting value. Imagine me with resolve and a strength beyond my years (at least, this is how I imagined myself). Imagine Randy with fourteen years more life experience than me but with an uncanny, similar determination to make the world a better place.

Now picture us peeing our pants on a scary playground.

When we arrived in Jackson, we quickly realized we weren't in our proverbial Kansas anymore. Any visions we had of our new field of dreams were replaced by the nightmarish reality of a church in upheaval. My first Sunday was the founding pastor's last. The staff was a mess. For some, flipping one another off in the halls and hurling insults at each other was the daily norm. While we knew in our hearts God brought us to Westwinds not in spite of the train wreck but because of it, we were shell-shocked. The tiny bit of courage and Holy Spirit wisdom we recognized in ourselves didn't seem to make it any easier for this bitter medicine to go down.

In the wake of the initial madness, we found ourselves doing different jobs than the ones we were hired to do. The church was broken, void of all its former recognized leadership, and was in a downward spiral. We listened to horror stories, passed tissue, performed triage, wiped butts, internalized threats, read hate email, had our vehicles keyed, discovered "anonymous" blogs that were written about us, endured name calling, and tried to protect our families from the onslaught of unwarranted garbage that sometimes gets slung by hurting people.

For months, we searched for a new senior pastor. But honestly, who would want to step into our cesspool? I looked at Randy Shafer one day and said, "I guess we lead this place." We realized God was doing something unique and it wasn't time to elect a new king. But what?

The next few months were the most spiritually, physically, mentally, emotionally (and any other "_____ally's" you can think of) draining months of my life. Easily. I resigned, un-resigned, gained 20 pounds, went through a severe depression, cried rivers, and ached for my family. All my leadership weak spots were exposed.

Then we met David McDonald and decided to hire him. Looking back, I often wonder what attracted him to our personal Dysfunction Junction. The church was barely breathing. Over half of the staff had left. David was a spirited, irreverent prankster with an immense love for Jesus and his Bride. He was also the most intelligent man I had ever met. It had to be Holy Spirit intervention. No one in their right mind would accept this poor job description, this small salary, this little power, and this much chaos short of God pushing buttons.

The three of us recognized something special was taking place with our relationship. It wasn't prescribed. It wasn't well thought out. It was just . . . unfolding. We decided to strap on our seatbelts and see where this ride would take us.

We adopted what we called a shared-leadership model. In this model (that existed only in our minds with nothing to compare it to) we would all make decisions together, dream together, plan together, lead together. No one person would have the buck stop with him. We had no idea what we were doing but it felt right. A new leadership model was forged partly out of the necessity for camaraderie, partly because of a shared story and new determination, and partly because of fear mixed with stupid optimism and a whole lot of Holy Spirit intervention. My favorite mantra during this time became one said by the character Jack on ABC's *Lost*. "Live together. Die alone."

To show how dedicated we were to the concept of shared leadership, we all moved in to one office together. We ditched our old titles and sought after a new name to mark this new thing we had no good way of describing.

Every pastor we met told us we were crazy. Businessmen in the church set meetings with us to tell us why it would never work. More blogs. More hate mail.

David's wife Carmel suggested the metaphor of the "Coriolis Effect" for our three-headed leadership monster. We did some homework and learned the Coriolis Effect, along with the uneven heating of the earth, is what causes wind. The Coriolis Effect is what makes a skater spin as she pulls her arms in tightly. We aren't physicists, but we loved the word pictures. Coriolis was born.

I had hoped that Randy and I had absorbed most of the collateral damage by the time David arrived but I was wrong. David walked with us through our pain and encountered new pains alongside us. We were all in this together. In the suck.

Our Coriolis of three became two after the death of our partner in crime, Randy, in 2008. We walked the road of evil cancer with him for almost two years. Randy's battle and his passing was the crest of the wave in a perfect storm that nearly ruined us all. Statistics say Westwinds shouldn't be standing. Statistics say we should be the sacrificial lambs. Statistics sometimes lie. Jesus says different.

Fast forward. Westwinds feels as healthy as any church I can imagine, which is to say we are a bunch of messed up people falling more in love with Jesus all the time. The old ghosts are gone. There is healing. There is new life. We're playing the long game.

I could not begin to talk about leadership and what I believe about leadership without giving you, in part, a brief and crude outline of the last decade.

In the next few pages, you will become acquainted with many of the stories that have shaped us over the last decade. We have strong opinions in part because of these stories. But please know, if you disagree with our individual assessment of our stories, we are completely okay with that.

This book is subtitled *Permission Granted* on purpose. If you disagree with me at turns, that's good. You might be getting closer to articulating for the first time some of the things you believe about the way you are called to lead. Or, perhaps you are confirming those things by disagreeing. Or, perhaps you start to rethink your position.

You might find that we articulate something in a way you have never been able to do. It's not necessarily because we're smart. It might just be that hearing someone else say something, in the way *they* say it, strikes a chord. That happens to me all the time.

Finally, much of my leadership philosophy was shaped in a foxhole and played out in a theatre of operations locked arm in arm with two of the best men I have ever served with in ministry. My ideas are David's ideas. His are mine. Randy's influence can't be underestimated and his voice still plays in my head.

David was originally planning to write this book with me but then he encouraged me to move forward without him. I can't write this without you understanding how much my personal voice is in many ways an echo of the collective voice of Coriolis. Bottom line, I didn't make this stuff up on my own. We don't know who coined what in this quirky philosophy. A lot gets done when no one cares who gets the credit.

CHAPTER ONE &
NECESSITY IS THE MOTHER OF PERMISSION

I'M NOT A "LEADER"

I have ideas. Good ones. As a matter of fact, part of what makes me good at what I do is that I think I can do most things better than other people can. I have just enough humility to know I am not perfect and just enough pride to believe I can do most things better than you. I know this is shocking, and you might not know me, so let me assure you I am being a bit sarcastic while exhibiting some self-disclosure at the risk of sounding like a self-righteous idiot.

All leaders have a bit of healthy confidence. Sometimes mine gets out of whack. This is why I have removed myself from the leader pool in the past or at least doubted my ability. After all, aren't leaders *always* supposed to be *perfectly* humble?

I've always been taught to believe that Christian leaders don't have that degree of confidence (pride) in themselves. They are big fans of creative collaboration and believe all God's children have a place in the choir—even (maybe especially) the ones who sing incredibly flat. But I don't necessarily believe that. This is one of the reasons I've never really fancied myself a leader.

This leads me to another observation about myself. Leaders use words like "fancied" in sentences. But I don't. Except for that time in the last paragraph where I thought I'd try it on for size. I didn't like it. I like to think I'm smart, but really, I think I'm pretty average (maybe a little above) on the smart scale. I've always been taught to believe leaders speak and write well, but I have never considered myself a natural scholar or orator. The times I sound good come with a ton of practice and hard work.

I have tattoos, a crazy beard, and earrings, and I like them all. Sometimes I wax and curl my mustache because it's fun. I even pretend my wife enjoys it too. I tried to wear Dockers slacks for a while, but I felt like I was being punished—like that time I had to write "I will not say that word" 1,000 times after I cussed out my cousin's dog in front of my mother. I tried the slacks (or trousers, as my grandpa called them) because I thought it was expected of a leader.

This is probably a really good time to tell you I think sarcasm is one of my spiritual gifts. Sarcasm is a powerful tool for

communication, and it sometimes gets me in trouble (often). The nature of sarcasm is that it speaks for itself—you don't always have to point it out. Until you put it in print form and serve it up to people who don't know you. Sarcasm comes from a word that literally means "the tearing of the flesh." When it goes bad, it goes horribly wrong. I pray that doesn't happen here. You'll get sarcasm in small doses throughout this book. This penchant for sarcasm has been a point of contention for me in my leadership, and sometimes it has been sin on my part. This is another reason I have second-guessed my calling at times.

I have a library full of leadership books. These books have much in common. They all have lists of things I am supposed to aspire to be as a leader. Some of the advice has shaped me. Some has enlightened me. Much has discouraged me.

I have been to leadership conferences. I have listened to countless leadership CDs (I started with cassettes), podcasts, and seminars. I've gleaned much from them. And yet, I have often come away thinking, "Who am I kidding?"

OR AM I?

I once thought a leader spoke a certain way, dressed for the part, always paid for lunch, enjoyed patent leather, and couldn't wait to get on the golf course.

This year, I finally decided I don't like golf. Sure, I like driving the cart, I like a beer after the game, I enjoy the conversation, and I occasionally hit something straight and feel the thrill. But I don't want to get any better. I don't dream about it. And it's kind of boring. Now, what kind of a pastor or leader does not like golf?

I'm not even joking about my leader perceptions. For years, I carried this burden of not measuring up. Then, one day some things turned around for me. One of the leaders I look up to (who tucks in his shirt) told me he wished he could lead like me.

Like me? I asked him what he saw in me that he wanted to aspire to. He told me he appreciated that I could speak my mind without being a jerk (most of the time), that people wanted to hear what I had to say, that people genuinely wanted to be on my team, that I exuded an incredible freedom and daring optimism, and that I got stuff done.

I think he just wanted me to buy dinner.

I do know this: I have ideas, creativity, opinions, and tastes that have been forged through opportunities and stepping in where things have been left undone. Most of the leadership positions I have held have been given to me in the wake of a disaster, a church split, or a major upset of some other variety. I've always been the next guy. In many cases, I've been forced to clean up the mess and forge a new way while mending wounds.

As such, I have a style and a leadership personality that has emerged through trying stuff on for size. I think what my friend really saw in me (because I am most definitely not all those things, even in my own mind) was freedom. Freedom to try. Freedom to fail. Freedom to do my best without a blueprint. Freedom to ask, "Who said we can't do that?"

I blow it all the time. People get mad at me often. But people do like to watch a fire burn. Freedom in a leader is a fire people want to be around.

I realize now I am a leader. Just not that kind. Or that kind. Or your kind. Or her kind. My kind. The kind God made (and is making) me to be and has shaped (and is shaping) me to be by his influence, life situations, people, experience, choices, education, and a myriad of other influences.

I have also realized something I wish every person in my position could realize, because it has been a gift: I may not fit the mold, I may not engage in the same water cooler conversations, and I may not frequent the same establishments as other leaders, but I have been entrusted with a group of more than 1,000 people in this particular franchise of the kingdom in Jackson,

Michigan. That is important. That is unique. That is who I lead. Not your church. Not his or hers. This one.

They are my people. This city is my home. I can't separate who I am from where I live. All leadership rules don't universally apply. All places are not my place, and all people are not my people. I'm not only a leader; I am this leader. Their leader. Now.

WHO ARE YOU?

If you are reading this book, you probably consider yourself a leader. Or you want to be one. Or you think you might be one. Or someone told you that you are.

Leadership can be an invigorating and fulfilling experience and call. It can also be maddening and lonely. It's hard to know if you are doing it right if you think you may be doing it wrong. And someone always wants to tell you how to do it better.

Usually, doing "better" in other people's minds means they have a good idea of how you need to change. Adapt. Become something else.

But how about becoming the best "you" you can possibly be?

What if those crazy ideas in your head are supposed to be acted upon? What if making that outrageous decision to do that thing people laugh at is one of the most important things you can do for your church at this time? What do you do when the proverbial wisdom is "there's safety in a multitude of counsel," but you and your leadership partner/team think everyone else is all wet?

This is not a book about what deficiencies you need to sharpen in order to lead better. This is not a book about discovering your holes and how to patch them. This book will not give you a diagram of the perfect leader who is someone other than you.

This book is about discovering who you are as a leader, remembering who and what you are called to lead in your specific situation, identifying the things that make you a unique leader in your context and culture, celebrating those things, and communicating them well.

This book is also not about building other leaders. It's a little self-centered. This was a choice on my part because I believe there is a myth in Christian circles that the best leaders spend most of their time building other leaders. While building other leaders is a stellar, worthy goal, this book is designed to be a path of discovery in order to give you permission and confidence to lead all those people by first understanding what the heck you believe about leadership.

WAS JESUS THE PERFECT LEADER?

"So, you want to be a leader? Just look at Jesus." That's what someone once told me. Quite frankly, I don't know that I necessarily like the advice. I mean, Jesus was mistreated, misunderstood, and homeless, and they killed him.

Often, people will want to use the Jesus card to help you determine whether you are making the *right* leadership decision based on a *similar thing* Jesus did. These are things I have heard regarding decisions I've made and what Jesus would have me do instead:

- Jesus never gave up on someone. You shouldn't stop counseling that person.

- Jesus had a group of 12 disciples. We should have small groups with no more than 12 people in them.

- Jesus drove out the moneychangers, so we should not have any money transactions in the church.

Did Jesus have the perfect size for a small group? I'm sure he knew what he was doing and 12 seemed the best number based on the people he selected and invited, but I'm pretty sure he could have gone with 11 or 13 if it suited him, and if he had picked 17, it still wouldn't have been prescriptive for us.

These silly out-of-context connections about what Jesus would do in our scenario based on what he did back then in his are ridiculous. All leadership scenarios require their own exegesis and innovation. Jesus certainly made good leadership decisions, but he wasn't giving us a leadership blueprint—at least not in these very specific ways.

As a Christian, I believe Jesus was perfect. He was perfect in the sense that he was everything the Father intended and spoke of from the beginning. He was perfect in his work on the cross, his victory of death and sin, lacking nothing. Complete. Fulfilled. The end.

But can we say he was born the perfect leader? The best communicator who ever lived? Was he innately the best at everything he touched?

This is where it gets tricky. And harder to prove.

Jesus was a carpenter (most likely a stone mason). Did he build the best custom homes?

When Jesus sang as he walked down the road, did people marvel at his angelic voice and call him the songbird of his generation?

Was Jesus always picked first for the basketball team because of his killer dunk shot and his ability to sink the three-pointer?

Jesus was human. Jesus had to learn things. He wasn't born talking. He filled his diapers, and he had to be taught how to tie his sandals.

If we say Jesus was the perfect leader, should we make that claim about his whole life, or just about his life at the end? If he was the perfect leader at 33, what can we say about 25? Or as a teenager?

Jesus must have had spiritual gifts like all of us. Jesus must have stunk at something, or at least have been mediocre at something. If this isn't true, we should stop telling people the church body is made of different parts and so they shouldn't feel bad about not being good at one thing over another. We should tell people they should become good at everything as Jesus was. See how weird that is?

If Jesus was innately good at everything, he wasn't human. He was a robot. A perfectly programmed robot with an operating system that never failed or had to be rebooted. The absence of sin should not be equated with the ability to excel at everything.

Jesus is perfectly God. But this doesn't mean he always won the foot race, made a perfect lamb meatloaf, or would win *American Idol*, *The Voice*, or *Chopped* hands down. I'm sure they would vote him off the island on *Survivor* no matter how well we think he could "Outwit, Outplay, and Outlast." They killed him, for crying out loud.

He, like the men of Issachar in the oft-quoted 1 Chronicles 12:32, understood the times and knew what he should do. He read the signs. He paid attention. He made decisions based on the context he was in and observed. He surrendered his will to the Father.

Knowing that Jesus read the signs, interpreted the times, exegeted his culture, and made the decisions he felt necessary to his context, as opposed to giving us a perfect blueprint for all kinds of leadership, should give us a new kind of freedom and permission to lead through all the unknowns.

LET ME ASK THIS AGAIN; "WAS JESUS THE PERFECT LEADER?"

The first time I asked this, it was in the context of universal schematics and diagrams. Systems and blueprints. Prescriptive methodologies without context.

This time, I want to ask the question based on character. Attitude. Perspective. Mission. And this time, my answer is a resounding "yes."

Jesus. The servant leader. Perfect.

Of course, the concept of servant leadership—attributed to Jesus—is not new to us. Libraries of leadership books have been dedicated to the concept of servant leadership, and I don't know that there are many books on "Christian" leadership that leave out this concept. It is good. It is Jesus' idea.

However, practically speaking, I don't know that we understand what he meant by it. Servant leadership is often bastardized and ghettoized to mean:

Having a sympathetic ear. Always. At the drop of a hat.

Being fully present. When anyone demands it. Any time.

Valuing other opinions. By assigning them equal worth.

Profit sharing.

Christmas bonuses.

A good human resource department.

Processing together. Until everyone agrees.

Brainstorming. Everything.

Seeking to understand. Until we change our mind.

Listening twice as much as we speak.

Speaking in soft tones.

A staff footwashing.

If these things are true of servant leadership, Jesus had some learning to do as a servant leader. Jesus should have a talking to in regard to calling people names, overturning tables, asking his mom why she was bothering him at a wedding, telling other leaders they were wrong, and going off to be alone when everybody wanted a piece of him.

He still had an opinion (John 5:44; Luke 16:13).

He still set boundaries (Luke 5:15–16; Luke 4:28–30).

He didn't allow people to manipulate him (Matt 12:46–50; Luke 23:8–9).

He sometimes put people in their place (Matt 21:23–27).

He preserved his mission (Mark 1:38).

He didn't let the power brokers have the upper hand (Matt 22:15–22).

He broke the social and cultural rules (John 4).

Being a servant does not mean surrendering opinions and tastes at all times (though it might at some). Being a servant does not mean being wishy-washy to make sure everyone's voice is heard. We have other descriptions for these traits, like indecisive, neutral, un-opinionated, and having no backbone—things that don't sound like leader qualities at all.

No one wants a team captain who lets everyone brainstorm and decide the game plan at half-court. No one wants a coach to poll the crowd. No one wants a president whose platform is "I'm not here to cause waves."

No matter where you are in the leadership hierarchy of your church, there can really be only one vision. This is not a book about defying your senior leaders or getting forgiveness as opposed to permission. Quite the contrary.

Servant leadership in Jesus' case led to his death. Laying his life down was ultimately what he was called to do, and nothing kept him from accomplishing that vision and mission. Competing visions were cast aside.

If you lead a team of people who really want ABC vision, but there is a leader who oversees you who clearly has XYZ vision, the answer is XYZ. It's not necessarily XYC (partly the leader's and partly yours sneaked in). It's definitely not XY and maybe they won't notice Z is missing (the leader's minus the part you omitted).

A leader certainly can and should value those they lead by entertaining other opinions. But he or she doesn't have to feel bad about XYZness—especially if XYZ is a clearer reflection of the vision the leader is called to protect. For the leader of leaders, death does not look like the surrender of XYZ when the vision is at stake. Death often comes in the course of *defending* XYZ.

Defending the vision is a full-contact sport. While vision "leaks" according to many leadership professionals, the leaking requires communicating "clearly, creatively, and continually," according to guru John Maxwell (p. 67). His book *The 360° Leader* discusses the many ways vision is challenged, from *criticism* and *sabotage*, to *ignoring* and *abandoning* vision (Nashville: Thomas Nelson, 2005). How does Maxwell suggest we "successfully navigate the vision challenge?" "The more you *invest* in the vision, the more it becomes your own" (p. 64). "*Participation* increases *ownership*" (p. 65).

Adapting to vision, *championing* vision, and *adding value to* vision (Maxwell's list of preferred responses to "The Vision Challenge") come with *investment* and *participation*. But never does Maxwell suggest surrendering the vision to others when you are the one called to champion it. Who would? Participation and investment require *people* to change. Not the *vision*.

Sometimes there's a need for compromise in little things. Sometimes there's a need for change and mutual understanding, leading to harmony of both slants. Sometimes a parting of the ways is in order. Sometimes servant leadership means cohabitating and submitting, but XYZ always prevails.

When I moved to Jackson, Michigan, I had a real good idea of how I would fit into the established structure. I thought I knew how to craft a weekend worship gathering based on what I thought I knew about the culture. But culture shock hit me strong.

It didn't take long to realize some of my established methodologies, personal tastes, and preferred ways of leading would not work in my new structure. I had a lot of ABC in me in this new XYZ. Everyone in Coriolis did. But we agreed that XYZ wins.

For instance, I wasn't a huge fan of country music, but my new town was steeped in it. I am, however, a big fan of a lot of music that has much in common with the brand of country they were listening to. It would have been tragic for me to force my favorite music down their throats and be contrary.

Instead, I started listening to a steady diet of some musical heroes who may not fit squarely in the country genre but rhymed with it. And I stretched myself to listen to some bands I would not necessarily choose for myself. Tapping into those influences and letting them flavor my own preferences not only helped me support XYZ in the way it needed to be, but it also gave my new family a confidence in me and the grace to even allow me to speak new influences into them from time to time. They allowed me to be me because they sensed my burning desire to find com-

mon ground even if it meant I had to die to some personal preferences. XYZ wins, and we all win.

CREATIVE COLLABORATION IS DUMB (INSERT ROOM FOR HYPERBOLE HERE)

I don't really mean this. But I do sometimes.

I've already described our leadership team Coriolis to you, in the preface, which is by definition a team of creative collaboration, so you know I don't completely believe the statement above. Sometimes hyperbole allows us to make a bold statement and de-power it all in the same breath. So where does collaboration go wrong?

I recently got a Facebook message from a friend in ministry. He had taken on a job as a pastor of a church in the West. He asked me for some advice on what he should be reading or listening to so he could bone up on some things that were way outside his comfort zone as a leader. He was getting a lot of pressure from some people on his new teams to lead according to the last guy's way of leading.

They were having meeting after meeting to get on the same page and carve out some creative options for the future of the teams. In these meetings, where nothing was getting resolved, everyone got to share his or her advice and ideas. They called it "creative collaboration."

But it wasn't creative. And it wasn't particularly collaborative. There was no seeking to learn from one another, building on ideas, brainstorming together, or progress. It was about trying to get your idea heard. Being the loudest voice. Or the most annoying. Many churches have these kinds of meetings.

My advice to him was simple. "Tell them your leadership style is different than the last guy's and you hope they will understand why you are doing things a different way." It is one thing to seek to understand and be sensitive to another's tastes and preferences, but it is a completely different thing to bow to the wishes of everyone on your teams and in your church. There is no need to apologize for your own style of leadership. Don't be an ass. But don't apologize.

Everyone has advice. Everyone has a personality. Everyone has a preference. Many of these things will clash with you as a leader. The people you lead will clash with one another. Allowing (or fostering) an environment where everyone is always heard (read "everyone has the right to tell you why something is wrong") is ridiculous. Someone will always be disappointed. It is not your job as a church leader to make everyone happy. And you can't. I tried for years.

Conventional wisdom says, "Everyone should have a voice" in a church organization. Meetings are set with people of all different personalities so everyone feels represented and that there is some sort of team camaraderie. The idea in these meetings is that we can "all learn from each other" as we plot a course. In some churches, entire staffs are built this way. Somewhere along the line, some of us bought a lie that it takes incredible diversity, with everyone speaking at the same volume, to build a healthy church staff.

Creative collaboration is a lofty goal, but someone has to lead. In my experience, way more can be done in a much shorter period of time when like-minded people dream together. Like-minded collaboration certainly leaves room for disagreement and sharpening of ideas, but it does so while everyone is heading in the same direction. Creative collaboration works *only* in the context of a central vision and relationships of mutual trust and understanding.

I'm not saying, "Never listen to anyone who has different ideas." But there comes a time in church leaders' lives when they realize what they like and don't like, the style that is theirs and the style they don't gravitate toward. The vision they are called to own. The methodologies they believe are wise. Leaders become very aware of the people who will constantly try to change them, the choices they make, and the way they lead. A leader must recognize this kind of antagonism as unhealthy for both parties. It is unhealthy for a leader to live under the weight of feeling compelled to meet everyone's demands, and it is unhealthy to let people continue to throw their weight around.

With our staff, we hope we have created an environment where people can share ideas and disagree, but at the same time, everyone must have a good idea of who we are and why we do things the way we do so that not EVERY idea is open for challenge.

The more you talk about why you do the things you do in the way you do them, the easier it is for a staff (volunteers, lay leaders, the rest of the church) to see inside your head as a leader. Challenges become less frequent. You will start to build a group of like-minded folks who are clear about where you are headed and how to get there.

Will the people you lead have opinions that are different from yours? Guaranteed. Will there be scuffles? Sure. Should every contrary opinion be given equal attention and weighed the same? Absolutely not.

MORE THAN ONE WAY TO SKIN A CAT

I know a guy who uses this phrase all the time. What he means is that there is more than one way to get things done. I've always liked this word picture because it is very appropriate for what sometimes happens when visions collide. It is messy. It is bloody. There is whining.

Of course, your way of doing things isn't the only way. Let's not be that pompous. But whether you have been elected, appointed, voted, commissioned, ordained, or selected, or you find yourself holding the reins asking, "How did I get here?" you have a responsibility to shepherd.

Gene A. Getz's book *Elders and Leaders: God's Plan for Leading the Church* is an insightful and thorough study examining biblical roles and responsibilities of leaders of all shapes and sizes. Getz says, "It may be surprising to learn that the biblical story of local church leadership offers little data to make the specific observation that someone must function as the primary leader" ([Chicago: Moody Publishers, 2003], p. 217). And yet, Getz explores all the places in scripture where there are "primary leaders" who evolve or are appointed, because "it's imperative that we have a *total biblical perspective.*"

Getz's study pays special attention to Peter as the leader selected and groomed by Jesus himself. He notes that Peter was already a primary leader in his "enterprise" of the fishing business with his brother Andrew and friends James and John when Jesus called him. Jesus then groomed this imperfect leader to be a decision maker (Acts 1:15–22), someone who would strengthen his "brothers" (Luke 22:31–32) and a shepherd (John 21:15–17), even to some who were also shepherds (1 Peter 5:1–3). Peter came from a long line of leaders and is part of a rich history of leaders throughout all scripture:

> It's God's design—from time to time He chose men
> like Moses, Joshua, Samuel, and Nehemiah in the

Old Testament, and Peter, Paul, Timothy and Titus in the New Testament—to always have a key leader in place to lead His People. Why would we think differently when it involves elders/overseers in a local church? (p. 223)

Churches have leaders. Regardless of the selection process or methodology that was used to appoint them, if they hold the title of leader, and everyone recognizes them as such, they must lead. It is a responsibility of biblical proportions, complete with qualifications (1 Timothy 3), warnings, and instruction (1 Peter 5:2–3; 1 Timothy 5:19–21). Paul calls attention to those who "direct the affairs of the church," saying they are worthy of "double honor" (1 Timothy 5:17–18).

Pragmatically, overseeing, shepherding, directing, leading, managing, and decision making (or whatever words you use to describe the functions of leadership) cannot be done void of opinion. You are paid, in part, because of *your* taste. Or, if you've been asked to volunteer for a leadership position, it may be because of your particular bent. If everyone expects you to be the leader, it has to be done in the way you have been shaped. In the way you see things. In the way you interpret things.

No one else wants to take the blame when things go wrong. They can't have it both ways. When you lead, you get the good, the bad, and the ugly fallout of your decisions. There is no one else to blame, and there shouldn't be. There is great satisfaction in knowing your ideas and plans have failed because of no one's fault but your own. This is very helpful for you in determining what to do next time.

My dad is a painter. A good one. He used to refinish yachts in the San Francisco Bay Area. He paints custom homes now and refinishes cabinets most of the time. My dad knows there is more than one way to paint a house. He has a crew of guys working for him who all have their own ideas and experiences of what works best. But my dad has his name (and reputation) on the side of the truck.

If my dad left them to their own devices, would they do a good job? Of course. They have great ideas. It's not the end result that would be tarnished in most cases; it's the skinning of the cat where things go awry. My dad has very clear ideas about what is right and wrong on his jobsite. It's his prerogative to have those ideas. He's the leader.

When rolling a wall with paint, my dad requires his workers to use a five-gallon bucket with a paint screen. They could use one of those square roller pans that sit on the floor, but my dad doesn't want them to. He requires them to use canvas tarps. They could use plastic, but he doesn't want them to. It doesn't matter who thinks something is "right" or "wrong" in these scenarios. My dad is the leader. The cat showed up on his doorstep.

We want to be good listeners. We want to try new things on for size. We want to hear new ideas. But at the same time,

there are decisions that need to be made without everyone's diverse input. Leaders must sometimes make decisions that are uncomfortable or unpopular with some. These decisions range on a continuum from *matters of taste* to *matters of life and death*.

Sometimes the fallout from those decisions is people saying things like, "This is supposed to run like a family," or "I thought we were all in this together." While these things are not entirely untrue, the metaphors of family and team break down at some points. Everyone wants to be "in it together" until they realize that means shared sacrifice, everyone taking arrows, everyone bearing ultimate responsibility, and everyone going down with the ship.

GAMES PEOPLE PLAY

This past year, David (my work wife) got on a kick and started collecting unusual chessboards and pieces. They look very cool. Some of the pieces are quite unusual. I especially like the themed pieces like the sea creatures that currently sit on his desk. But my intrigue with the themed pieces is as far as my love for chess goes.

David thought it would be fun to have an ongoing game in our workspace. Because he is my friend, I agreed. We take turns on this game whenever we feel like it. We have a prop we move from one side of the table to the next to remember whose turn it is next. The prop usually sits on my side of the table for days. And weeks. Until David says, "Hey man, it's your move." Then I feel guilty and take a move.

I'm not a chess pro or natural by any means. It is often frustrating to me. I sometimes make dumb moves. A player has to think not only of the next move, but also of the moves that are going to happen after that as well. I have to guess sometimes based on what I think David is going to do. I have a loose overall game plan, but that plan has already changed a few times.

When this current game is over (and if David pulls another guilt trip on me), we will start another game. It will be different. I will learn from the first game, but the landscape will change and I will have to think differently. On my feet. With loose, new strategies. And a willingness to adapt. I'll take the information as it comes, assess it, interpret it, and move forward. There are "rules" in the game, but there are many different ways to play it.

Quirky leadership is a game of chess. I know metaphors break eventually, and you will probably find a few holes in this one. Good. At least you're thinking, evaluating, and forming opinions. That's what you're supposed to do.

I see a hole in this one too. When I ask, "What are my chess pieces?" I understand some of them are people. Real people. With real opinions. And I certainly don't want to be a puppet master, controlling and manipulating people to do my bidding. Just so we're clear, it's the voices of those "pieces" that can help us win the game together. They can also interpret and see things from a different angle as they move around the board. Still, when the game is over, the people who are counting on you to play the game well are not going to blame bad decisions on the rook.

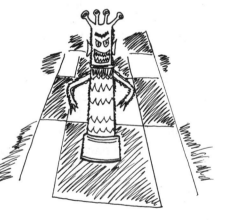

It's your move.

CHAPTER TWO:
YOU'RE SO QUIRKY (YOU PROBABLY THINK THIS CHAPTER'S ABOUT YOU)

Pastors and ministry leaders have deep-seated beliefs about the way ministry should be done. Life experience, schooling, books, relationships, mentors, and reactions against any number of situations and examples where there was "bad" leadership shape those beliefs. Those strong beliefs don't always translate well in the day-to-day decisions we make. Sometimes a leader will passionately make a decision about something that seems trivial to the people he or she is leading. In turn, the people being led will sometimes respond by being passive-aggressive, by writing their leader off as "opinionated," by labeling their leader a control freak, or by feeling like they will never understand or live up to their leader's expectations.

We have a lot of talks with our staff about the way "we" do ministry at Westwinds. A lot of our talks have come out of discussions and reflections on *plumblines*. Plumblines are a concept we first heard about in Larry Osborn's book *Sticky Teams*. In construction, a plumb line is used to measure verticality, depth, and the center of gravity. We like to think of plumb lines in terms of our personal bents, preferences, and even quirks in regard to "doing" ministry. And David and I (my partner in Coriolis) have a few of them. According to Osborn,

> Plumb lines don't represent the only way to do ministry. They represent your way of doing ministry. So don't worry if they seem somewhat narrow

or controversial or even if they thin the herd. . . . If forced to choose between a great mission statement and a clear set of plumb lines, I'd choose the plumb lines every time. That's because the devil and most disagreements are in the details. (p. 153; 157)

I lead a group of artists, scholars, entrepreneurs, and monks—to name a few. They all have individual styles. They all have ideas. They have their own ways of getting from here to there. Some are processors. Some are busy bees. Some are mellow. Some are prepubescently hyper.

Then there is me. I have a lot of deep-seated beliefs about art, ministry, leadership, aesthetics, music, media, and church life, with more than twenty years in professional ministry and a lifetime of stories where things worked or didn't work. My job—along with David—is to look forward, change, take the temperature of our church, read the signs, be aware, influence momentum, point the way, and cast vision. Besides the more lofty leadership things, in large part, we are paid for our taste.

Somewhere along the line, we realized not everyone on our staff knew our plumblines. Some beliefs about ministry are lodged deep within us, and they influence our decisions but don't always translate well. So sometimes we might passionately make a decision about something that seems trivial, a little quirk someone might write off as "That's just John. He's opinionated." Or, "That's just David. He's a dork." In reality, there is often deep meaning behind even the little decisions.

At best, our plumblines are inspiring, influential, exciting, and educational. But we are also aware that some of our plumblines can be interpreted as silly quirks unless you know where they come from.

For instance, if you come to me with a homemade poster you drew with magic markers and you want to tape it up on the bathroom wall at church, I will tell you no. I have a deep-seated, rock-solid opinion that this is very tacky. On the surface, this seems trivial. No one is being kept from coming to Jesus because of homemade posters. However, this is all part of a plumbline I have that is very meaningful and well-seasoned.

On our list of plumblines, homemade posters fall under #16 on our list:

#16 EVERYTHING SHOULD BE DONE WITH EXCELLENCE AND CARE ✓

If we were on a group field trip and had a deadline and destination, we couldn't just leave each to his or her own way, or we would eventually get separated, give up, get lost, change course, and maybe end up hating each other. On a group field trip, someone needs to herald the route and the schedule. That's the role of Coriolis (shared leadership) at Westwinds. That may indeed be your role as a leader.

GO TO QUIRKY LEADERSHIP .COM TO SEE PICS OF WESTWINDS

Our plumblines are more than mission, vision, and values— they are the rules of the road. Our staff members know, hold these up, and pray these plumblines will help us ensure that our ministries, decisions, and initiatives align with the core values and priorities we claim to have. And they let everyone know how we're supposed to do things around Westwinds. They don't represent the *only* way to do ministry, or even necessarily the *right* way to do ministry, but <u>they do represent *our* way of doing ministry</u>. Their purpose is to clarify how *we* plan to shadow God, build the church, and heal the world *right now*.

BEING AN "AGENT OF CHANGE" IS NOT FOR THE BOOK CLUB

I have a few friends in book clubs. I've never been a part of one. When I asked one of them what they do there, I was told they "talk about the book they are reading, discuss their favorite parts, tell life stories that the book reminds them of, talk about the parts they didn't like, make fun of some things, and share opinions." That sounds a lot like some of the church boards I've been part of.

I asked my same friend if he is part of a Bible study. He is. I asked him how the Bible study differs from his book club. "It's not much different," he said. "Except we don't make fun of things or really talk about the things we don't like." His Bible study operates within the rules of what is known as "reader-response criticism." This school of thought puts the reader at the center of the literary work. The book is interpreted based on the reader's individual experience and feelings. And, in this school of thought, one cannot divorce the interpretation from that individual. So in a group setting, a book can really be about anything. Meaning is unique to the individual.

I have always found this a dangerous Bible-study model. But it is the most popular. I've been to countless Bible studies that are run by individuals whose task as the leader is to ask, "What was your favorite part?" or "What does this mean to you?" or "What do *you* think Jesus was saying here?" The responses are most often varied, and seldom does anyone challenge the individual interpretations brought to the table. I have a deep-seated belief that the Bible means something. It has multiple layers of depth and meaning, but that isn't the same as meaning *all* things or *any*thing.

Reader-response leadership can be dangerous in a Bible study. Sure, everyone can have an opinion, guess at meaning, fill in the gaps of the story, or talk about life experience and how they were affected by the reading. That's not where the problem lies. Those things can be helpful if we are all trying to arrive at truth and meaning. But any good biblical scholar will tell you meaning lies in the context of the whole of scripture. Meaning is not dictated by opinion or feeling when it comes to scripture. To interpret scripture, you read in context. You cross-reference. You seek to understand the author's intent. You take into consideration the original audience. You examine the cultural setting. You determine the genre and don't bring the interpretive rules of another genre into the one you are focusing on. You submit to the rules of grammar, poetic device, and literary structure.

Many of these same rules apply to leadership. At the end of the day, good decisions and bad ones will be determined by how well the leader interpreted the signs and was immersed in the context of what he or she leads. Times change. Needs change. Technology changes. Culture changes. Leaders must watch and interpret these changes for their context. They must create their own change as well. If you consider yourself an agent of change but operate in a reader-response format, you are fooling yourself.

Opinions can be helpful. There is often safety in a multitude of counsel. Other people have better ideas than you do from time to time. But having our decisions dictated by whoever wields the sword of greatest persuasion or has the strongest opinion at the time is not wise.

The metaphor of reader-response leadership breaks down if you hear me suggesting there is one right decision at any given time and the leader must make it. I am not saying that. I am, however, saying that while there may be many decisions that can be the *right* one, someone has to make it. And that person must not let peripheral things unrelated to the context sway that decision.

You'VE BEEN GIVEN PERMISSION

If you are a pastor or leader in a church, you have been given permission to lead in your context. The people who hired you gave you that permission and, quite frankly, God did as well. Of course, this is a responsibility rather than a right.

I'm assuming we all agree that just because someone is in a position of authority, it doesn't make him or her respectable, honorable, or credible, or grant innate good character. I am also assuming we all agree these traits are things we work on with the help of the Holy Spirit as we daily die to ourselves and make mini-surrenders all over the place. For the sake of this one-sided conversation I am very thankful you are listening to, let's both assume you are a leader who measures up as best you can. You are a follower of Jesus. You know you are not God. You are respectable and have good character. You have flaws, you are aware of many of them, you learn new ones all the time, and you strive to put God first in everything you do. There is no grievous unconfessed sin in your life. Your family is in order. No one is saying you are perfect, but all things considered, you are a normal, broken, trophy of grace. And you are the leader.

If this is the case, and it is with many of you, with your responsibility comes permission. It's God's idea. He wants you to experience freedom in your leadership. He certainly wants obedience and holiness, but you are not His puppet on a string leader. God has always given leaders freedom and permission in their responsibility. Not permission to do "any" thing, but certainly permission to try anything within the boundaries of what is godly and wise.

You are given permission to lead the people with whom you have been entrusted according to the vision and dreams God has given you and the way he has shaped you. Depending on your role (unless your title is Pastor of Fulfilling Others' Dreams),

God most likely did not call you to see other people's dreams to fruition.

So you see inside my head: when I refer to vision, I am most often referring to the overarching plan, structure, personality, and makeup of your ministry—the things that don't change much over time. When I refer to dreams, I am most often referring to the specific, time-sensitive, project-based, missionally oriented "stuff" that you do at your church. Dreams are held up against the vision. Vision is held up against the mission. Jesus gave us the mission in Matthew 28 (even though we often change the wording of that mission to fit on a t-shirt, which I have no problem with as long as the meaning doesn't change). The mission doesn't change. The vision changes less often. The individual dreams change constantly (or should).

The first evidence we have of permission in decision-making is with Adam in the garden. Work was always part of God's plan for Adam (work wasn't the curse). Working and tending the garden was part of who Adam was and part of the role he fulfilled. He was given authority over the birds, fish, and animals. He was given much responsibility, and he was given choices. He could freely eat from every tree in the garden. Just not *that one*. Of course, he blew it. He tainted it all. We still do.

The freedom and choices Adam was given were not taken away with the curse that followed his bad decisions. Life from then on was going to be painful for humanity, but the choices still remained. In many leadership and decision-making scenarios, this is a good rule of thumb. Garden theology says we can make any number of choices and still remain in God's will. We just can't make *that choice*.

I heard an imaginary story once about Adam and Eve deciding what to make for dinner after *prayerful consideration*. In this story, they wanted to make the right decision, so Adam went on a prayer retreat while Eve stayed home and prayed. When they got together, they didn't have an answer, so they went back to praying. They discussed at length. They weighed pros and cons. They so badly didn't want to get it *wrong*.

The point of the story was that God did not supply for them a perfect dinner choice. He put them in a garden full of choices. All were good. Except for one. He told them which one they *shouldn't* pick. This imaginary scenario is typical of the way many of us approach God's will for our lives. It's the same kind of approach that some people have when they are looking for a job or a spouse. Some believe that God has sanctioned a *perfect* choice for them.

However, we can find no clear evidence in the Bible that God makes a habit out of revealing a perfect choice for us through prayer. Some choices are better than others. Some choices are definitely wrong. There may be any number of choices and visions we could pursue in life that may be *inside of God's will* for us. When it comes to making choices, we can know some things with absolute certainty:

> God will not move us to do anything contrary to scripture. His word is his revealed will to us (Psalm 119).

We can also safely operate by the proverbial ideas:

> There is safety in a multitude of counsel (Proverbs 11:14).

> Being open to correction is a way to wisdom (Proverbs 19:20).

Choices can be made in light of his word, counsel, and wisdom. You can pick any job in the world—just not *that one* (for example, the job is making pornography). You can have any spouse who may reciprocate your love and your wooing—just not *that one* (for example, the object of your affection hates God and everything you stand for).

In many ways, the OT prophets were "tested" by this logic and this instruction. When they said, "Thus sayeth the Lord," they were opening themselves up to the testing and scrutiny of scripture and of the community (Deuteronomy 13; 18).

In reality, we are seldom faced with the kinds of "false dreams and visions" that Deuteronomy warns about, though history has shown the church and the world abroad plenty of "crazy" visions and schemes that, left unchecked by scripture and wisdom, have ended in tragedy. Kool-Aid anyone?

However, countless seemingly harmless ideas and visions are presented to the local church all wrapped up in a box stamped "God gave me this vision" day in and day out. Often, people judge the validity of their dreams, visions, choices, and ideas based on the lack of any apparent obstruction or difficulty in achieving them. In the same way, many are quick to judge something as invalid or *not God's will* based on roadblocks.

Scenario: A man is out of work and applies for a job in a new town. His wife hates the town, they will have to compromise on the children's education, they have been warned by many friends not to go there, the man has a history there that will be hard to overcome, there is no church for them to be involved in, etc. However, the man is offered a new position in the town after searching for work for a year. Should he take it?

Scenario: A woman applies for a job in a new town. She has been drawn to this town her whole life. Though she has been gone a few years, she grew up there, there is opportunity to help the community, she loves her home church there, and she has many great relationships there. Many have counseled her that it would be wise to pursue something in this town. She knows that if she keeps pushing on toward her dream of moving back she can accomplish great things, and she has a vision for the community. But she can't find a job there. Should she give up trying?

It is my conviction that just because something comes easy, it doesn't make it good. And just because something is difficult doesn't make it not worth pursuing. Life as God intended us to live it is nothing less than an adventure. It comes at great risk and at significant cost. Jesus summarized it like this in Luke 9:24: *"For whoever wants to save his life will lose it, but whoever loses his life for me will save it"* (NIV).

Based on the multiple passages like this one where Jesus talked about surrender, yielding our lives, adventure, and service, it is not a difficult leap for us to surmise that God-sized vision and dreams include a degree of faith and risk. The most important thing is understanding who has ownership of the initial risk.

Wise counsel and scriptural congruence are a must as a measuring stick for a vision or dream. My co-pastor David and I like to define a dream in this way: "the intoxicating burden of your ambitions to shadow God in the redemption of the world." This is the easy part. People can usually jump on board with wanting God's stamp of approval. It isn't always hard to ask friends to weigh in on the wisdom.

Where it sometimes gets tricky in the church world is when people take that vision to leadership and want their church's stamp of approval and help (or the office's, or the family's). Often, people get frustrated or give up because

"No one understands me."

"No one understands this burden."

"No one sees the validity."

"No one has passion like I do."

"The leadership is not tuned in to this problem."

"The leadership doesn't care about this."

"There are too many hoops to jump through to make my vision happen."

When we dream something, we invest a lot of emotion and energy into thinking about it. We wouldn't bring it up if we thought it was a dumb idea. But the barriers may lie with some basic erroneous presuppositions that people sometimes have about vision and dreams in the church.

Erroneous presupposition #1: "My vision or dream should be everyone's vision or dream."

The answer to this misconception is "No, it shouldn't." We really don't even need to search scripture to prove this. Common sense and history tell us this is so. Dreams and vision don't work that way. But for some reason, people in the church and church staff often approach their particular vision this way, whether they state it or not.

It's unfair. To everyone. To the dreamer and the final decision-maker alike. Every church has a personality and style. Not all churches' personalities are fit for an individual's vision, or vice versa. Such dreams—pursued in the way the dreamers see them—may either compromise the style of the churches or cheapen the dreams, or both.

Church leaders have a specific vision or dream within a community that takes priority over other dreams. We don't apologize for this. It doesn't negate other dreams or visions; it just means they may not be right for our particular church. *That* person and only *that* person may be the one God has raised up to fulfill that vision. And it may be fulfilled somewhere else. There is not enough time or money to pursue everyone's dreams, even if they all measured up.

Erroneous presupposition #2: "The church's job is to come alongside me and make my dream or vision happen."

While sometimes the church leadership may embrace a dream that originates with an individual and decide to support it on a "grand scale" (read: promotion, time, money) because it seems good and right for the season, it is not the "biblical" role of pastors and elders to live out the dreams of individuals. Rather, it is the role of the leadership to provide counsel, direction, wisdom, and teaching that enables individuals to test the validity of their dreams and live them out. Ephesians 4:11–13 says:

> *It was he who gave some to be apostles, some to be prophets, some to be evangelists, and some to be pastors and teachers, to prepare God's people for works of service, so that the body of Christ may be built up until we all reach*

31

unity in the faith and in the knowledge of the Son of God and become mature, attaining to the whole measure of the fullness of Christ. (NIV)

Erroneous presupposition #3: "There are no bad ideas or dreams if they are selfless and God-focused."

This is where wisdom and counsel come into play. The fact is, there are bad dreams or, at least, unwise ones. There is bad vision. There is misplaced vision. There is out-of-context vision. There are contradictory dreams.

Dreams may only be unwise for a time. They may have holes. They may need time and energy and investment to come to fruition. They may be a waste of time. They may distract someone from the priorities God has already laid out for them. I am convinced that one of the tools the enemy uses to get us off track is to whisper in our ear, "You are not doing enough for God." Often, we dream things that may be valid and even earth-shattering but decide it would be wrong for us to pursue them because of our current time, priorities, and commitments.

Sometimes, a dream needs to be tabled for a while. Certainly, dreams worth dreaming take work—again, on the part of the dreamer. Paul urges us in Romans 12:1 to offer our selves as "living sacrifices." This is worship. Dreaming can be an act of worship. Pursuing dreams can be worship. Surrender is always part of worship. Therefore, surrender is always part of dreams.

Sometimes dreams are very spontaneous and time sensitive. Sometimes, they need shaping and honing. The Holy Spirit that moves spontaneously in us and through us is the same Holy Spirit that guides us in making wise choices, planning, and setting goals. Our legacy, for some of us, will be how we trained our churches about pursuing dreams and God's view of what lasts and what has value. Our churches need a spiritual dream ethic.

Mistake: Church funds people's dreams → People dream → People give those dreams to the church leadership → The church leadership lives out those dreams.

Truth: Church funds people's dreams → People dream → The church authenticates people's dreams and coaches them → People do the hard work of living out their dreams.

BEING SENSITIVE AND BUSTING THROUGH

I was watching *The Sound of Music* one day with my daughter, Kasidy, a few years ago. At one point, Maria the nun said (I think it was Maria), "When God closes a door, he opens a window."

"Is that true, Daddy?" Kasidy asked.

Sorry, Maria. I don't agree. I can't tell you how many times I have sat with that freaking door closed, wondering if God is going to begin to chisel through the wall at any minute and install a nice vinyl-framed escape hatch. It has never happened *consistently* that way for me.

It has happened before. I have been headed in a direction I was sure God was leading me in, just to find a closed door. Then I saw another opportunity to take advantage of. I like to think it is God having my back. But it doesn't always happen, and God never promised me he would spare me from pain. He did promise me a lot of hard work and tears, however. Yes, he never leaves us or forsakes us, but hard work and tears are for sure.

At times we are surrounded by walls—maybe ones that are closing in on us. No window. No door. No light. No escape. I don't blame this on God. Sometimes I blame it on myself. While God is not always there with a chainsaw to carve out my window, I also don't believe that God chooses to abandon me there.

I think God calls us to kick down doors at times. To burrow through and under walls. To bring on the black powder. He wants leaders. I like to think of the door-kicking scenario like you sometimes see in the movies where the sweaty, dusty, exhausted hero finally finds a crack in the wall or the secret piece of the puzzle that breaks down the wall in the desolate cave to the treasures beyond it.

But I need to temper this, lest you think I am proposing hedonistic humanism. Another misunderstanding I have picked up in pop culture came from Michael Landon in an episode of *Little House on the Prairie* that I was watching with my daughter. This was the episode where Pa told Half-pint that "God helps those who help themselves."

While the Bible teaches hard work, the sweat of your brow, preparing the future and anti-sloth, it doesn't claim we don't need God or that dreams are achieved only through hard work.

God helps those who can't help themselves.

God uses others to help those who can't help themselves.

God uses us in spite of ourselves.

God doesn't need us to get things done.

God is not powerless to move without us willing him to do so.

We need God's help. We need to rely on him.

And . . .

We need to work hard. We need determination.

We need each other. We need the church.

We need wise counsel. We need checks and balances. We need instruction.

We need to dream. The world needs dreamers. The world needs follower-leaders.

When we dream and pursue dreams, we imitate God. In a good way. Like children imitate the good things in their parents.

One of my favorite passages of scripture is found in Nehemiah. The walls of Jerusalem had been destroyed by King Nebuchadnezzar and remained that way for about a century and a half. Fear and apathy held the Israelites back from repairing the walls completely, though they tried.

The prophet Nehemiah was a dreamer. A leader. And a man who loved God—a follower. The book of Nehemiah gives us a picture of Nehemiah the prophet weeping over Jerusalem and the state of the city and its walls. Many scholars agree it was not the condition of the walls that burdened him as much as it was the Israelites' failed attempt to see the rebuilding through to fruition in the face of opposition.

The Bible tells us Nehemiah left his post as the cup-bearer to King Artaxerxes to stir his people and inspire them to rebuild the city walls of Jerusalem with the blessing of the king. This would have been a prestigious position to leave behind even for a time, as the cup-bearer was more than just a servant. He was one skilled in fine wines who had the honor of working close to the king. It was a position of favor.

Leaving the job, however, was not the risk or hard work of seeing a dream to fruition. This was a minor inconvenience. The risk and hard work came in knowing that all the enemies of Jerusalem did not want the city walls rebuilt. The walls left the city open to attack. The rebuilding of the walls would once again make Jerusalem a hard-to-penetrate fortress and a powerful adversary.

The passage that inspires me and scares me at the same time is a beautiful picture of what a dream and leadership can cost us:

So I stationed armed guards at the most vulnerable places of the wall and assigned people by families with their swords, lances, and bows. After looking things over I stood up and spoke to the nobles, officials, and everyone else: "Don't be afraid of them. Put your minds on the Master, great and awesome, and then fight for your brothers, your sons, your daughters, your wives, and your homes."

Our enemies learned that we knew all about their plan and that God had frustrated it. And we went back to the wall and went to work. From then on half of my young men worked while the other half stood guard with lances, shields, bows, and mail armor. Military officers served as backup for everyone in Judah who was at work rebuilding the wall. The common laborers held a tool in one hand and a spear in the other. Each of the builders had a sword strapped to his side as he worked. I kept the trumpeter at my side to sound the alert.

GO TO
COMMON ENGLISH
BIBLE.COM TO
READ ALL OF
NEHEMIAH
4

Then I spoke to the nobles and officials and everyone else: "There's a lot of work going on and we are spread out all along the wall, separated from each other. When you hear the trumpet call, join us there; our God will fight for us."

And so we kept working, from first light until the stars came out, half of us holding lances.

I also instructed the people, "Each person and his helper is to stay inside Jerusalem—guards by night and workmen by day."

We all slept in our clothes—I, my brothers, my work-men, and the guards backing me up. And each one kept his spear in his hand, even when getting water. (Nehemiah 4:13–23, *THE MESSAGE*)

Of particular note is the picture of common people fighting for a dream working with tools and materials in one hand and a sword in the other. That dream was cast by a quirky leader and seen to fruition by a quirky leader. A leader who felt permission to say, "Who says we can't do that?"

I wish it went without saying, but it doesn't: the best leaders are followers. Leaders are given permission to follow. To listen to the Spirit. To follow his lead. To make any number of wise and quirky decisions as you follow the One who is clothed in humility.

CHAPTER THREE:
I KNOW WHAT I KNOW
IF YOU KNOW WHAT I MEAN

Every time leaders are faced with a decision, we are making a choice between ease and dis-ease, peace and conflict. Many times, leaders will choose *ease* and *peace* because conflict is hard and messy and exhausting. But the net result of choosing ease over dis-ease and peace over conflict is that we end up with *everyone else* leading our churches.

Even those with the shallowest beliefs about church leadership believe God has called them to lead in that place for that time. If that is true, you must understand God knew what He was doing when He chose YOU to lead.

To lead effectively in only the way you can, you need to go through a process of determining what is worth fighting for. The truth is, some things *aren't* worth fighting about, and sometimes leaders choose to fight about the wrong things. Sometimes leaders choose to fight about the right issues, but we're on the wrong side of them. We need to tell these things apart from one another and, once we define them, embrace them, no matter how insignificant they may seem to someone else.

PLAY TO YOUR STRENGTHS

No one person has to have a corner on the leadership market. Conventional wisdom regarding leadership strengths and weaknesses says this:

1. Listen to others.

2. Survey yourself.

3. Identify your weaknesses.

4. Work hard to remedy those weaknesses.

But I'm not sure this is entirely helpful. God's goal is not to clone everyone. If you are good at making widgets (let's give you an A-) but horrible at making gadgets (let's give you a D-), the energy it takes to sharpen your skills as a gadget artisan is exhausting and counterproductive.

You will most likely hate yourself and everyone around you in the gadget-artisan honing process, and I'm not entirely sure you will ever be satisfied with the results. You make crappy gadgets now, and the difference between your D- gadget and even a C+ gadget may cost you your family, your sanity, your friends, your staff, some respect, hair loss, and a few pounds from stress eating multiple bags of Chili Cheese Fritos (or, your own stress-snack of choice). Why?

No one person can possibly possess all it takes to make widgets, gadgets, thingamajigs, and whirligigs. We are made different for a reason, and leveraging your energy toward your strengths is optimal.

How do you recognize where you're strong?

- What do you do that doesn't feel like work?

- What energizes you?

- What do you find yourself talking about positively all the time?

- What do people compliment you on?

- Where do you find you add most value?

How do you know where you're weak?

- What demoralizes and discourages you?
- What constantly slows you down?
- What do people always want to fight with you over?
- What makes you want to quit?

I have a friend in ministry who was exhausted every time he went to visit someone in the hospital. He wasn't good at it. He hated the atmosphere of the hospital, always felt awkward, never knew what to say to the sick, prayed the same prayers over and over and felt bad for it, and found himself failing in other areas because of the time it took for him to be successful in visitation.

One day, someone told him he was foolish and no one should expect him to visit all of the sick in a church with two thousand members, even if he *was* the senior pastor. Instead, my friend was advised to do what he did best: recruit, train, and encourage new leaders. He instantly began putting together a team of people who can out-love, out-pray, out-cry, out-sympathize, and out-empathize anyone in the church. They spend all their time visiting the sick.

The sick are better served. My friend is now able to continue doing the things he does well, and as such, the entire church is better served. He now jokingly lives with the motto, "If you get a visit from our team in the hospital, know you are very loved. If you get a visit from me, know you are very sick." His whole church understands this and applauds it.

Of course, when I talk about focusing on your strengths at the exclusion of weaknesses, I am in no way talking about ignoring moral deficiencies and character flaws. God wants to shape you, mold you, prune you, and change you. Like making a canoe, He wants to take you and carve away everything that is not Jesus in you. I'm also not giving leaders an excuse to be lazy or accomplish their work with a bare-minimum effort.

Bruce always showed up late to meetings. Always. He would even lie about why he was late to church meetings. When confronted, Bruce said, "It's just part of who I am. You're going to have to live with it." His senior pastor disagreed and finally fired him. Being late may have been part of who Bruce is or was, but that was a weakness that got in the way of all his strengths. It weakened people's opinion of him. It was an excuse and a character flaw.

I'm not excusing Bruce when I talk about not needing to be good at everything. I'm talking about skills. Aptitudes. I'm talking about your self-absorbed dream of perfection (and mine as well). How many things do we need to be good at? How many trophies must a leader have? What skills does God require you to perfect?

I have a few friends who are professional students. Continuing education is wonderful and staying sharp is important, but these friends' motives are different. These friends have been preparing for ministry for fifteen and twenty years in some cases. They have multiple degrees. From multiple schools. Not to mention multiple dollars in student loans. For some of them, I wonder if they will ever get to a point where they believe they have *what it takes.*

What is it that drives a leader for perfection in every area? Pride? Maybe. But sometimes they are driven by a lie that has been engrained in them—the lie that a leader must be *all things to all people.* When the Apostle Paul talked about being all things to all people, he in no way, shape, or form was talking about sharpening his skill sets. Paul adapted, paid attention to other cultures, and made sacrifices with his preferences and customs to be able to relate to others. Paul was motivated by others' best interests. Unfortunately, some have misconstrued this either consciously or subconsciously to think they should or even can be awesome at everything. It's exhausting. It can't be done.

When I was finishing my undergraduate work at Multnomah University in Portland, Oregon, I took a class on the minor prophets. The professor was a favorite of mine. He was a dynamic communicator and a moving storyteller. I wanted to make him proud and excel at everything in his course. I don't think I got lower than a 97 percent on any assignment.

At some point during the semester, this professor called me into his office. I knew I wasn't in trouble because I was doing so well. He looked me in the eye and said, "John, you have a 97 percent in my course."

"Yes sir, I do!" I said proudly.

His next words floored me. "I'm disappointed."

I gasped and wondered how in the world anyone could be disappointed in me. I was excelling at everything he put in front of me. I was one of the best students in the class.

That was why he was disappointed.

He told me he knew what it took to get that kind of a grade in his class. He knew the kind of dedication and sacrifices someone had to make. I was a married student with two kids at the time. I was a pastor at a church. He said, "So, tell me. What's suffering?"

He saw right through my façade. On the outside, I was a stellar student impervious to the big, bad world of academia. I could juggle everything two men could juggle. On the inside, I was crumbling. My marriage was suffering. And quite frankly, though it was a Bible college, Jesus had barely any of me. I was too tied up with being all too perfect.

He asked if I would give him permission to show me how to get a C+ in his class. It was a passing grade, and "average is not bad." I settled on the path to a solid B+. He showed me what assignments to skip and how to study in order to pass. Together, we identified what assignments took too much of my time. He taught me that sometimes the cost of the difference between a B+ and an A+ is a family.

If you try to lead like the Ultimate Fighter, something will suffer. Surround yourself with people who accommodate your deficiencies and allow yourself permission not to be A+ at everything you touch. Tell your team what your weaknesses are (they may know them already), and give them permission to rise to the occasion without feeling like they are stepping out of line.

A leader who has weaknesses exposed and allows others to lead in their areas of strength is a leader who will be respected when laying down the law. A leader who gives permission for others to lead according to their strengths receives reciprocal permission to be the leader he or she is called to be. A leader who acknowledges he or she is less than perfect is seen as a human being and is more likely to be heard.

Leaders who spend time majoring on the minors and trying to be perfect in every area often surrender their energy without fighting for the things they really believe in. In the long run, squelching the things we really believe in takes its toll on us in much larger ways—stress, burnout, cynicism, apathy, disdain for ministry, and even hatred for those we lead. Where you are strong, be strong. Where you have conviction, speak boldly. Where you have experience, shine.

So what do you already believe about leadership? What are your convictions—no matter how big or small? What mountains are you willing to die on?

You're Right

Okay, not all the time. You certainly make mistakes.

But when it comes to leading our churches, I'm amazed at how much time is wasted on the wrong battlefields of taste and style. Certainly, everyone has particular bents and preferences. It's hard to make a case for who is right and wrong in a battle of taste. However, if you are the leader and you are creating and protecting the culture of your church, you get to be right.

In many churches, the fear of being an autocratic leader keeps people from getting anything done. In the spirit of creative collaboration and diversity, many organizations find themselves in a perpetual state of processing and talking about one another's feelings. We don't do our churches any favors by being wimpy and indecisive. Identifying and celebrating our quirks is not the gateway to communism or being un-American (and I'm not certain autocratic leadership is as evil as it's made out to be).

Even biblical go-to models of leadership are often misunderstood. We have great biblical freedom in "how" we lead. The metaphors in scripture are more concerned with our hearts. For example, *servant leadership* does not mean *allow people to walk all over you and do whatever they want*. Even "shepherds" don't allow the sheep to graze wherever they want. We need to differentiate between attitudes and methodologies.

We do our churches and co-leaders a favor by celebrating our quirks. They are frustrated when they have to guess what we want. They want to understand why we say "no." We can celebrate creativity, diversity, freedom, and permission, but we don't have to be afraid of well-defined boundaries, preferences, and styles. Being right doesn't mean being a jerk. Being right doesn't mean flaunting your power. But being right absolutely means you have the final say.

Recently, I read an article that mentioned James Cameron changed the appearance of the nighttime sky in one of the scenes in his epic "Titanic" when he released it in 3D in 2012. He changed it because an astronomer pointed out the sky was not technically "right" for the Atlantic sky at the particular time the Titanic sunk. The constellations that a character was staring at were all wrong. She would not have seen those stars on that night.

That was a brave move for Cameron. He admitted he was "wrong" with the sky scene, even though it looked perfectly "right" to an audience who didn't really care about what the sky looked like in that particular scene. We were captivated by the drama, not the particular artistic license that Cameron took.

That was a change he was willing to make. His movie. His prerogative. But multiple websites list numerous other things that Cameron got wrong in his made-for-screen adventure. For instance, cameras are seen in mirror reflections, and beauty marks move from one side to the other side of the cheek between scenes. Hairstyles change within the same scene.

But were those things really *wrong*? Sure, people with too much time on their hands were able to find all of Cameron's mistakes, but what was his goal in making the film? Was it to have everything *right* according to everyone's specifications? Was it to be historically accurate? Or was it simply to tell a monumental story and win our hearts?

How does this relate to leaders in ministry? You are going to make decisions in the best interest of the kingdom that could be based on intuition, wisdom, wise counsel, input from other overseers, biblical precedence, sensitivity to the Spirit's leading, an awareness of shifting culture, timing, or all of these things put together, and those decisions may not be *right* to everyone. You'll delete footage (cut a program). You'll accent certain scenes with more dramatic music (give more attention to something from the pulpit). You'll create spin-offs (add new campuses). The choices may be wrong to some. Even then, you can still be right.

Sure, we need to be editable. But not in all things. In matters of character? Yes. Morality? Yes. Style, vision, branding, staffing, programs? Not necessarily. Someone is going to believe it is right for your church to worship for two hours on Sunday as opposed to the hour you believe is right. Someone is going to believe you shouldn't sing a particular song or style of music in your church. They think it's wrong. You are going to love that same song. Some are going to believe you should never fire anyone on your staff because it is not nice and the church is a family. You are going to hate firing that person but know deep in your heart it's right for the church.

Sometimes, the leader will be the antagonist in the situation—at least that's what the person you oppose will see you as when you say "no" or "not yet" to them. Sometimes your "no" will feel like a personal attack on them because you have labeled their thing, their idea, their personal mission as "wrong." Maybe not sinful. Maybe only for such a time as this. But "wrong" nonetheless.

Leaders who have strong opinions about vision and the flavor of their ministry have many crossroads moments with people over time—moments in which tough decisions are made and the potential to break a relationship in the process is strong. Leaders need to walk lovingly through these times but not necessarily cautiously. If you are a leader, lead. Love as you lead. Listen as you lead. But lead. Sometimes the protagonist says no. And it's the right thing to do. Sometimes saying "no" is just saying "yes" to a bigger "yes." Sometimes saying "no" values someone else's "yes."

When I was a kid, my spiritual mother told me that God always answers prayer. Sometimes He says, "Yes." Sometimes, "No." Sometimes, "Not yet." God has different reasons for all those answers, but He always answers with our hearts in mind. He sees the bigger picture. We certainly should not be equated with God in this scenario, but can't we learn from Him in this? Does He not want us as leaders to have the best interest of the kingdom and all His people in mind?

Sometimes, choices are not a matter of biblical right and wrong. Context, culture, level of engagement, back story, history, vision, taste, timing, and appropriateness are just a few things that can affect a leader's decision making. When you are the decision maker, it's okay to have an opinion. You count. (Some of you have denominational leadership structures or know that you will never ultimately be the leader who has the final say, which makes these claims seem lofty. I promise to address your concerns in a bit.)

PORN WEEKEND

It was the right call. But man, did we pay for it.

It was the right decision, but it came with a bloody nose.

It was the right idea, but we learned some painful things through the execution of it and the fallout of the loose ends.

I'd still do it again.

Shortly after I arrived at Westwinds, I sat in a room with some of the staff talking about the big issues in our community. One of our staff members brought up the problem of pornography among students at our local college and how it was ruining their lives. Another part-time staff member was counseling quite a few people who were addicted to pornography. That led to other conversations about people in our church who were affected (and infected) as well by what XXXChurch.com was calling the "Dirty Little Secret" in the church.

We started asking our *professional* people around Westwinds (counselors, teachers, law enforcement) to share their stories about this little-talked-about infestation. The stories were bothersome at a deep level. Porn addiction was causing way more damage than even what we imagined. Our people were losing jobs. Pastors were blowing their churches apart. Students were failing school. Some addictions were leading to men taking advantage of women in horrible ways as they played out their fantasies. Some were in jail because of it. Others hadn't been caught yet.

Within a short period of time, we decided we needed to do something about this epidemic that no one else seemed to be talking about in church. We called the guys at XXXChurch.com and asked them to speak at Westwinds on a weekend. It was during this conversation that we learned Mars Hill Church in Grand Rapids, Michigan, was doing a similar thing with the XXX guys. God's timing was perfect.

We arranged for XXXChurch to come speak at Westwinds immediately after Grand Rapids. We decided to call it "Porn Weekend." We didn't want to mess around with naming conventions that lightened the impact of this serious problem. Men in our church were getting divorces after their wives walked in the room (on many occasions) and found them with their pants down while watching women (and in some instances other men) engage in sexual romps. I refused to call it "Jesus Wants Your Heart" weekend.

It was porn. It sounds dirty. Because it is.

The problems and controversy came in a few different waves. The first issue had to do with placement of some billboards we chose to erect (*wink*) around town. We rented space for new billboards around town that said "Porn Weekend" along with the name of our church and website contact info to learn more.

Little did we know that when we purchased billboard rental space, we would not be able to choose the location of those billboards. We got what was available.

In front of an elementary school.

Across from a day care center.

Across from another church in town.

As soon as we found out, we called the sign company to take down the ones by the school and day care center and find other locations. But it was too late.

The phones rang continuously. We got hate mail. We had picketers. We got threats. The television show *A Current Affair* called me and asked to interview me and come to Westwinds to cover the weekend. Our local newspaper printed an article that was so void of facts it was almost humorous. It claimed we would have a thirty-foot inflatable penis at the church on Porn Weekend.

The placement of the billboards was only the spark that ignited a fire that would have started anyway. The placement of the billboards wasn't the wisest decision the sign company made, but in all honesty, there are signs all over our town and littering our highways that are far worse. One of the billboards opposite ours was using a half-naked woman with her tongue hanging out to advertise a product, and no one complained about that.

And here's a strange thing indeed: we didn't receive any calls or get any threats from anybody other than Christians. Angry Christians. From other churches. Angry Christian home-school alliances. Angry Christian pastors.

What were they angry about? It wasn't just the placement of the signs. I promise. It was the fact that we said the word "porn" and advertised we were talking about it. We were told repeatedly, "Church is not the place to talk about pornography."

I beg to differ. If not at the place where people come and gather to respond to God, celebrate Him, and fall more in love with Him, then where?

Here is the one thing I could apologize about in the whole scenario: I am sorry we didn't get the signs down fast enough. I don't think it was wrong, but it wasn't wise. The principal of the school called to talk to me. He was kind. He had our back. He understood and was forgiving. I wish I had nice things to say about the people who keyed my car.

I am not upset in the least or apologetic in any way for making religious people angry. Porn Weekend had a phenomenal turnout despite the picketers (by the way, I think I recognized one of them from the picket line in front of a Stryper show in 1986). We had a handful of satellite groups start that were dedicated to beating porn addiction. We had men and women reconciling and finding forgiveness in their marriages. We had young ladies stop stripping in local clubs. We had brave women who stepped forward and asked for help letting everyone know porn is not just a man's problem. We had staff members ask for help in combating temptations.

Some may think Porn Weekend was too risky. Some may think you should never upset the Christian community and should always stay away from controversy. But I don't want to (and I don't think you want to) be a leader who gravitates to the lowest common denominator.

We've talked about doing something with Porn Weekend again. I like the concept of "Porn Again" for a billboard. I'll just make sure we get to pick where it goes.

Sometimes making the "right" decisions means you will lose friends. Sometimes the right decision means being called names. Sometimes the right decision breaks all the rules you've come to know. And sometimes, in the middle of all the fallout, redemption screams for joy.

You have been given permission to read the signs and act. You have been given permission to meet needs in ways that no one else has as you invent ways to connect with your community. You have been given permission to answer the call through the way God has shaped you as an individual and as a church. When fear and tradition hold others back or make them militantly scream, "No!" you have been given permission to say, "Who says?"

PERMISSION STARTS HERE

To lead effectively in the specific ways God has shaped you in your specific culture and circumstances, there is a necessary process of discovery in determining what you already believe about leadership, ministry, church, and mission:

1. Know Your Story

2. List Your Labels

3. Identify Your Quirks

4. Publish Your Plumblines

5. Celebrate It All

KNOW YOUR STORY

When did ministry begin for you? When you got hired at your church? Nope. Back up. Your entire life has been one of ministry, whether you knew it back then or not.

Even before you were a follower of Jesus, you were collecting details and ideas, learning lessons, forming opinions about people, developing a work ethic (or lack of one), and honing beliefs about culture and communication. You were storing up hurts that one day Jesus would deal with or is still dealing with. You were creating habits that may or may not have been good for you back then, and you're still waiting on the verdict for some of them now.

You have a story, and it affects the way you minister to people, make decisions, and evaluate risk. Your heavy baggage, your entertainment choices, your skeletons that are scratching on the inside of closets begging to be set free, your transparencies, whether you prefer to live life as a country mouse or a city mouse—God wants to use it all.

You have a story about how you started to trust in Jesus. It affects the way you talk to people to this day. You've seen people abuse the church and the church abuse people, and those stories affect the way you participate in (or ignore) conflict resolution. You have stored up stories, personal and observed as a bystander, of redemption and failure and everything in between, and these stories affect the perspective you have about people fighting the same demons and their ability to rise from the ashes.

You have stories about what has worked and not worked, what you're willing to try again, and what you are willing to kill someone over if it is mentioned again. You have tender spots in your personality because of experiences that, when grated upon by certain people, irritate you to the joints and marrow of your being and exhaust your will to live.

You have happy stories of battles won. Contagious stories of community victories that energize you and those around you when you tell them. You have an internal timeline, like a metaphysical Facebook collection of photos and posts, where the seemingly mundane has become part of your personality.

You need to know your story. You need to tell your story. The more you know it, the more you'll realize how it affects you. The more you know it, the better equipped you will be to handle numbers 2 through 5 on this list. The more you know your story and share it, the better people will understand you as a leader and follow you as you follow Jesus. The more you know and communicate your story, the more like-minded people you will meet along the way. Like-minded people are a very good thing when you are forging new territory, fighting against the system, and prevailing in the trenches against all odds.

LIST YOUR LABELS

How do people describe you? Not just the nice words. How do they describe you to others when they are talking behind your back? I'm sure you know.

Sometimes those labels sting.

Sometimes they hurt deeply.

Sometimes you want very badly to defend yourself against those labels.

Some of those labels might be flattering.

Some you are indifferent to.

To lead effectively in the ways God has shaped you for your particular mission field, you should be aware of how people describe you. To be quite honest, some of the ways we are described by others can point to a root problem of sin we need to deal with in ourselves. We're not allowed to write off our ungodly misalignments as part of our personality. Sometimes our personality traits and the way we carry ourselves and communicate with others is not necessarily sin, but we can still be off-putting.

Labels are often placed upon us when people don't understand us. When they don't know us well. When they don't know how we think or what we believe. When they are afraid of us or uncertain about our motives. Knowing our labels can help us communicate better and speak to all those gaps.

MY LIST OF LABELS

1. PERFECTIONIST   8. ~~   15. ~~
2. HARD WORKER   9. ~~   16. ~~
3. FUN   10. ~~   17. ~~
4. STUBBORN   11. ~~   18. ~~
5. ~~   12. ~~   19. ~~
6. ~~   13. ~~   20. ~~
7. ~~   14. ~~

A word of caution: we need to be editable, but do not *count* criticism as a leader. <u>Weigh</u> it. Not everyone's opinion counts. Contrary to popular opinion, there is not something to be learned from every criticism someone gives you. Some people reserve the right to be mean and judgmental. They don't count.

The opinions that ultimately count are the opinions of the people you have invited into your life to edit you. Some criticism is not helpful. But the kind of criticism that comes inside of a trustworthy relationship can shape and hone our waywardness into something beautiful as we invite the Holy Spirit to change us. The labels others place on us, filtered through the sieve of people with whom we are in relationship, can be of great benefit to us in helping people see inside our heads as leaders.

Wendy is a nice person who has been labeled many things that aren't nice. When she stands in front of a microphone and opens her mouth, it's a bit awkward sometimes. As such, she's been *labeled* gruff, not passionate, scary, and self-centered. But the people who know Wendy know this is not the case at all. They have been able to get to the root of some of the awkwardness. In reality, Wendy is scared to death. Her editors have helped her sharpen her public address skills so that she comes across differently at the microphone.

She has the same fears when she is speaking one on one with someone. She is unsure of herself and afraid. Her editors have helped her become a better leader by walking alongside her and loving her through stretching times. They are honest but not harsh.

Wendy has an incredible story. Telling her story many times over and talking about her fears has changed many people's perceptions of her. In reality, Wendy hasn't changed a whole bunch. Her microphone issues weren't sin. People around her understand her better now.

Mike is charismatic. He leads music at his church on the West Coast, but he is an East Coast transplant. He is loud. He laughs a lot. He quotes a lot of scripture—not as a weapon, but in the context of public worship gatherings. He has an East Coast style about him that screams SoHo. Even though he bought all his clothes at a thrift store in the village, he looks a bit flashy to some. Some call him arrogant. Some call him unapproachable.

In reality, Mike is one of the sweetest people his friends know. They would tell you he is kind, sacrificial, easy to talk to, and very, very confident in himself. Not prideful, just confident. Mike's confidence is not sin. But by seeing how he is perceived by others and having their harsh words filtered through the lens of his editors, Mike is better able to communicate with people and is misunderstood less these days. He also has a brilliant story of God shaping his life and lets people have a front-row seat to his story, complete with a healthy bit of self-disclosure. His stories have made him human. His stories have even made him attractive to the naysayers.

They call Frank a control freak. He really isn't a freak. But he is a take-charge guy, and he's not real good at delegation. His father taught him to be very self-sufficient and to pay attention to detail. As such, Frank gets a ton of stuff done as a leader. He develops brilliant plans. He sees great projects come to life. Sure, he's involved in a ton of it. But is that really bad?

Many will tell you that in order for Frank to be a good leader, he needs to work himself out of a job and train others to do the things he does. They will say Frank isn't sharing. They will say Frank cares only about the things he starts and finishes. But they are wrong. Frank is a caring, driven, passionate, talented, handy dreamer. Not only that, he knows how to move things along. I know many churches that would love to have him on their staffs. These are all great qualities in Frank. He treats people very kindly.

Knowing how he is sometimes perceived, his co-leaders have gathered around him in support. Some have taken the lead to support him by drawing attention to the great things he is doing without him having to tell the stories. When he was given an award by his township's board this summer, the other leaders in the church brought it to everyone's attention. When he created an after-school program for literacy, it would have been completely acceptable for him to announce it to his church, but he let his associate pastor do that. These days, Frank's achievements have been interpreted as wonderful examples of seeing a dream through to fruition.

Listing your labels is a great way to start identifying your quirks.

Identify Your Quirks

Before you state your plumblines, you need to identify your quirks. Your quirks are those things that are easily misunderstood and passed off as pointless matters of opinion or your way of communicating your dominance. They are your tastes, likes and dislikes, pet peeves, opinions, and prerogatives.

Think of it this way: if you have studied inductive Bible study methods, you know it is an important step in the interpretive process to observe. *Observation* is the part of Bible study where you—you guessed it—observe the obvious things within a passage. You make lists of repeated terms, phrases, and poetic devices. You pay attention to sentence structure. You determine what genre you are reading based on the literary clues. You examine the text for feeling, mood, and tone. You put yourself in the author's shoes. Perhaps one of the biggest disciplines of observation is training your eye to see. Observing takes a lot of hard, detailed work. Observation requires taking notes.

Identifying your quirks is much the same. Observing the fine print of your life and ministry and listing all of the things you have a particular take on should be quite revealing to you. You should surprise yourself with your list of quirks. If you don't surprise yourself, you need to spend more time observing.

Here's how quirks are observed in an everyday, mundane, non-ministry related situation:

You go through the drive-thru at your favorite locally owned restaurant on your way home after a late-night staff meeting. You order a diet drink, fries, and a veggie burger. You pay with a coupon you clipped from the paper and a few rolls of pennies. You make sure you say thanks to the people at both windows and fist-bump the cashier. You ask for extra salt and pass the drink holder back through the window to the cashier. You park in the parking lot and quickly eat your meal before heading home.

You don't feel particularly quirky. You don't feel like a weirdo. But you definitely have opinions and habits in this scenario. You sit down after that meal and decide to make a list of the things you know to be true about yourself based on your restaurant experience.

- "I like to support local business as opposed to chains."
- "I always buy the healthy choice but allow myself to splurge a little."
- "I still believe in buying the paper. I like the way it feels."
- "I save pennies like I'm still twelve."
- "I say more than the average customer at the drive-thru window."
- "I seldom salt my food, but I ask for it just in case."
- "I like to make the restaurant people happy. I think their job might suck, and I want to be nice to them."
- "I hate containers of any kind. Especially plastic."

- "Driving while eating is something we don't do in our home."

Not everyone thinks like you. Or acts like you. Or goes through the same decision-making processes you do. But I guarantee these specific little quirks play out in other areas of your life. There are bigger principles behind your quirks that are engrained in you that steer these tiny choices you make. They are part of your worldview. The way you see the world needs to be communicated to your staff and the people with whom you do ministry.

How might these quirks play out in your everyday ministry?

- When your assistant orders sandwiches for the next meeting from Jimmy John's instead of the sandwich shop owned by the wife of one of your teammates, you might get angry.

- When someone chooses to buy something that's not on sale, you might get angry.

- When the youth have a meeting and order one thousand non-biodegradable Styrofoam cups, you might get angry.

Your quirks influence your ministry and leadership more than you realize. You don't need to apologize for them, but you do need to recognize them. And you need to own them.

What are your quirks? What are your personal tastes as a leader? You have two choices when it comes to personal taste: you either let it all go and let someone else make the decision, or you stand your ground and call the shots. If you choose to exercise the first option, it's unfair to punish someone after the fact because you don't like what decision they made. If you choose the second option and lay down the law, it's good to be able to substantiate why you think that is the best decision.

Growing up, I always hated it when someone told me "because I said so." But the older I get, the more I understand the validity in a statement like that. Sometimes things need to be done a certain way just because you said so, even if you validate your reasoning as a matter of personal taste. Someone needs to protect your brand, your systems, your ethos. There needs to be some kind of standard. If there's not, something catastrophic will happen along the way where you are called to undo something someone has done, and a lot of feelings will be damaged in the process.

When we sat down to list our quirks some time ago at Westwinds, we came up with a list of more than one hundred things. Wow. That's quirky for sure. But, after closer examination, we were able to see patterns and group our sound bites into categories.

PUBLISH YOUR PLUMBLINES

If identifying your quirks is like the *observation* part of inductive Bible study, your plumblines are like the *interpretation* part. If we were studying scripture, after we've made all our observations, we would start putting pieces together to get to the big ideas. The interpretation of scripture is where we determine the timeless, universal principles and intended meaning. In much the same way, your plumblines are the grander things you believe that influence your quirks.

Spend time grouping all your similar quirks into like categories. Think of them as you did that junior high bug collection you did in science class. When they are all categorized, ask yourself, "What do these quirks say about what I believe?" In our food example, one of your quirks was that you saved all your pennies. You also recognized you hate containers—especially plastic. You might determine from both of these quirks that you have a deep-seated belief that:

59

Waste is irresponsible and ungodly.

You spent a lot of time spreading good cheer with the restaurant workers. You picked a local restaurant, as is your habit. You might determine you have a conviction that:

We are called to invest in the people of our community.

Both of these larger principles are plumblines for you. Other people may just see your idiosyncrasies and funny choices as quirks, but they are so much more than that. Our quirkiness (yours and mine) stems from convictions that steer our every tiny choice.

To help you prime the pump a bit in this process of quirks to plumblines, let's take a look at some real quirks we have at Westwinds and see what plumblines we arrived at. These may ring true for you as well. We have such a deep conviction about these leadership principles that we wrote them (scribbled, drew) on a wall in our office to remind everyone what we believe. We found it very helpful to include a paragraph description of these leadership principles when listing them for our staff.

Plumbline #1: What You Do Flows from Who You Are

For any idea/project/dream, the leader has to supply a truthful vision of the future. The leader has to go deep inside him or herself and figure out what he or she wants and why and how in order for it to work. If any idea is truly worth following through, it must come from somewhere. It must come from within the leader—the person who is willing to sacrifice to see the idea birthed into reality.

How did we arrive at this plumbline? We thought through the countless experiences we had where people tried to get *us* to do *their* half-baked ideas and how furious they got when we didn't respond with overwhelming gratitude when they presented their *thing*. We listed all the funny ways we feel about things churches sometimes do that are unproductive and overdone.

We thought about all the conversations we've had with people in which we told them that such-and-such was not going to be something Westwinds supported. We listed all the things we've tried and are bored of because they lost steam. We thought of all the trouble our staff gets into by delegating an idea to someone else who doesn't have the same passion. We thought about the horrid and time-consuming things our staff took on to make someone happy because that person happens to volunteer a lot of hours. We went down memory lane, told our stories, and listed our quirks:

We hate bake sales and car washes. They're overused ideas, generally not productive, and not creative.

We don't like doing what other churches do just because it worked for them.

We don't gravitate toward drama or showing movie clips on the weekend as a regular part of worship.

Plumbline #2: Everyone Gets to Be Who They Really Are

People should be treated like individuals. God made us each unique, and that uniqueness should be celebrated. To that end, we embrace our idiosyncrasies (pipes, tats, comic books, hanging at the pub, sci-fi, etc. are all in-bounds). We are comfy in our own skin. We want all people to understand that God wants them to become the best possible version of themselves, not cookie-cutter imitations of someone else.

How did we arrive at this plumbline? We have many quirks that fall into the *dork* or *nerd* category. We draw pictures in our

Bibles. We collect tobacco pipes whenever we visit somewhere or celebrate a monumental occasion. We have tattoos that tell stories of our family and church life. We go out after elder meetings and have a beer every once in a while. And we like it that way. We won't get into petty arguments about the validity of this or that when it comes to artistic expression or food, drink, and entertainment choices. Some of our funny quirks behind this plumbline:

We hate Dockers and dress shirts.

We think Comic-Con is a better choice for a church conference than many of the conferences being held today.

We cringe at labels and are not seeker sensitive, seeker targeted, postmodern, emerging, emergent, or any other label available to church culture.

Plumbline #3: Leverage Passion toward Responsibility

Staff members must focus first on their paid responsibilities. Whenever we have a passion that falls outside of our job description, we have two choices: either ignore our passion, or find a way to use that passion and bend it to our job. We don't want staff to ignore their passions, but we need them to do their jobs first because that's what we've decided needs to be done in order to move the church forward into the future.

Many times throughout the year, our staff members will have creative ideas they want to act upon, and they have to come to the crossroads of their dream and this plumbline. No one wants to be the boss who kills the staff member's joy, but no one wants to be the boss who doesn't have a productive staff, either. Over the years, our environment of freedom and creativity backfired on us many times as we tried to rein staff in to do their jobs. Do your thing. But do your job.

Kyle is a graphic designer. And an artist. And a dreamer. And an entrepreneur. And a self-starter. Kyle likes to start side businesses. He likes to develop helpful technology for people like iPhone apps and software. He wants to get paid for all these things. Maybe he should, and maybe one day he will. But Kyle was hired at his church to develop and maintain a website. Period. Kyle has some helpful skills for other areas in which he was not specifically hired, and occasionally he utilizes those skills at the request of his boss, but it's clear what his job is. Website.

However, more often than not, Kyle misses deadlines for web development and maintenance. Recently, there has been a lot of unpleasant conversation between Kyle and his boss. His boss is angry that things are not getting done. Kyle feels like he is not appreciated. No one notices the extra hours he spent at work helping the children's pastor get the security system up and running. No one thanked Kyle for the really cool app he developed for the iPhone that enables people to find out what is happening at the church quite easily. Kyle's boss never even mentioned how beautiful the new wall mural looks in the lobby that Kyle helped with on a Saturday.

Maybe Kyle's boss should be a bit more sensitive and observant of the wonderful things Kyle is volunteering his time for and thank him for being a great part of the church. But Kyle's boss is not the issue when it comes to Kyle's job getting done. Kyle is dropping the ball.

Recently, Kyle told his boss he wanted to expand his job description to include some of these other things he was doing. Kyle's boss told him no. When Kyle heard this, he raged a bit. He called his boss ungrateful and insensitive. Kyle's boss politely told him he was out of line. He told him he was thinking about letting him go if things didn't turn around quickly. In response, Kyle made a list of the things he was doing to help the church.

It isn't that Kyle's list wasn't impressive. It's not that Kyle's skills are not valued. Kyle is likeable most of the time, and everyone knows he's super talented. But

- Kyle isn't doing his job.

- Kyle needs to understand the difference between paid responsibilities and volunteer endeavors.

- Kyle doesn't get to choose what he gets paid for.

- There are a lot of people doing wonderful things at the church. They are not all paid employees. They are called Christians.

Kyle has some options. He can move on and take a job more suited to him somewhere else. He can do the job he's paid for and use the remnant of his energy to serve in volunteer capacities. He can swallow his passions and do nothing with them (hopefully, he doesn't choose this).

Or Kyle can find a way to incorporate his passion for all the various things he does to make the most amazing, comprehensive, accessible, monetized, artistic website ever owned by a church. This is what he's paid for. This would fulfill Kyle and make his boss happy.

Everything can be ministry, but *everything* is not necessarily what someone is paid for. (Pssst . . . I'm not letting myself off the hook here. This isn't just about the people who work under the leadership of someone else. As a lead pastor and a creative, I have found it helpful to surround myself with people who can edit me and speak wisdom into how I spend *my* time.)

As a leader, you can help the Kyles on your staff by dreaming about how they can incorporate their gifting into their job without distracting them from the job they are paid for. You can help them decipher and log their volunteer hours. If you ask them to do something extra for you, you would be wise to let them know it is outside their job description and is just a favor. Some of our quirks that helped us identify this principle:

We're bothered when staff members think they should be able to change their job description to include their new passion.

We don't think sitting at your desk dreaming about the way things can be can always be counted as productive work.

Just because you have a creative position at the church does not mean everything creative fits into that position.

All people should volunteer at least ten hours a week at their church. Even if they are paid staff. Where are you sacrificing?

Plumbline #4: Sacrifice Precedes Reward

Leaders are bleeders; they care so much they'll give their lives for the ministry. Whenever we look for leaders, we should look first to those who are willing to prioritize kingdom work at the expense of less-crucial concerns. The rewards for this kind of sacrifice include influence, position, and possible employment at Westwinds. This is one of the key ways we celebrate the virtuous, the noble, and the faithful. We have a very low tolerance for anyone who plays the victim card and has a spirit of entitlement in ministry.

We have an opportunity for many college interns and young people to work with us at Westwinds. Some are completing degrees in ministry areas such as worship arts. Some are going into the business side of ministry. Some want to be youth pastors.

Over the past ten years, we've seen a growing trend for people who are young in ministry not to want to work. To complain a lot. To talk about boundaries. To view ministry as a part-time job where they work only when it feels like they are able to use all of their narrowly defined spiritual gifting. Quite frankly, it's maddening.

When we first started in ministry as volunteers, we worked extremely hard for the sake of the kingdom. We sacrificed personal time and broke a sweat. We have little patience for the jobless kid whose parents are paying for him to go to school part-time, who drives his new car to our office to put in just enough time to get his teacher to sign off on his required ministry experience hours.

In some cases, we've hired interns who did a great job at one point in time and then turn a corner and act like the church owes them something. We have no tolerance for people who make demands while carelessly using words like *boundaries* as an excuse for not doing something they don't like or don't feel like they signed up for.

My friend once said his father (who is a pastor) told him everyone in ministry is required to eat one big bowl of crap a day. It's part of the deal. You eat it down. Sure, no one ordered the bowl, but they got it anyway. This is life. In the words of John Lennon, "Life is what happens while you're busy making other plans."

Yes, we feel a little raw when anyone has a spirit of entitlement and no work ethic. The person we want to hire as a youth pastor is the one who volunteered for years doing whatever he could to help out. He cleaned closets. He mopped up vomit. He volunteered in the areas that weren't always kid specific because he's a team player. He changed poopy diapers in the nursery a few Sundays. Without complaint. Sacrifice precedes reward.

When examining my own list of quirks, I realized just how big this one is for me. It may be for you as well. This is what I wrote down:

You are not allowed to use the word boundaries *with me unless you are over forty, married with kids.*

Your volunteer commitment is just like a job. You wouldn't call your boss to tell him you aren't working unless it was an emergency.

Don't ask me how little you need to do to get by.

Showing up late is a character flaw. It's not a personality thing. You don't get to blow it off or excuse it. Fix it.

Plumbline #5: Ministry Is Predicated on Relationship

Everything we do as part of Christ's church is relational. Authority is relational, not positional. Pastoral care is relational, not educational. This is why we want our staff to play well together. This is why we keep short accounts.

This is why we practice open and honest communication, speaking clearly and getting straight to the point. As leaders, this is also why we need to work hard to give everyone a chance to start over. Others may choose to hold people in bondage to their past mistakes. We can be aware of the past, and may sometimes choose to lead differently because of the past circumstances of our volunteers, but most important is the fact that no one ever gets shamed.

Some of my personal quirks that led to surfacing this principle:

I'm attracted to the unlovely. I like the freaks, weirdoes, unlucky, ugly, strange, and cape-wearing people.

I don't correct anyone or allow anyone to correct me unless we know each other. Well. I don't take kindly to criticism from strangers.

Music should be fun first and technical second.

It's okay for staff to have a margarita during a lunch meeting. The "rules" that would inhibit us are for corporate America. I don't like it when the church is run like Microsoft. If anything, we want to look more like Pixar.

Plumbline #6: God's Will Has Great Latitude

We have an incredible amount of freedom in choosing how to do the things God has placed within us to do. To speak plainly: God doesn't care what we do; rather, He cares more about what's happening inside us and through us than about what we're doing for Him or for others. Discernment is just as much about deciding what NOT to do as it is about figuring out what to do.

I love Rick Warren. He has greatly influenced me. He has influenced many church leaders. His books *The Purpose Driven Church* and *The Purpose Driven Life* have had great impact on the church in the last few years. But when choosing a movie or dessert option becomes *Purpose Driven* for people, I want to scream. I don't think that's what Rick intended.

When staff members ask "Why?" at the rapid pace of a three-year-old, it can be taxing. Communicate well. Sure. Explain. Absolutely. But sometimes you are going to have to make a call as a leader that is foreign to some, and they won't understand. Ever.

Steve was a staff member for a short time at my friend's church down the road. He's a great guy, but my friend says he was the most annoying staffer they ever had. Every plan that was unveiled by the leadership was investigated by Steve. Every staff meeting came with one hundred questions. Steve wanted everything to be explained. He could not live with any tension whatsoever. He had a militant need to seal the deal and fully understand before he could support an endeavor.

Steve believed it was his God-given responsibility to question. He admitted he didn't trust the leadership fully and believed they may have ulterior motives. Everyone is entitled to his or her opinion, but Steve quickly became a cancer on the team. He sowed seeds of doubt. He couldn't rest or be happy with an answer like, "We don't know how it will work, but we are going to try it."

One particular time, the church started an extended worship service on a Saturday night. They felt like it was something they wanted to try. They were reading the signs, and the timing felt right. Steve protested to no end, not because he thought it was a bad idea, but because the leadership didn't give a good enough answer for why they thought it was a good idea. Steve reluctantly and halfheartedly followed through with his part of the deal.

Six months later, the staff decided to cancel the service. It didn't produce the results they thought it would. Steve was once again angry. He wanted to know very specifically why they thought it wasn't working. At the end of the whole ordeal, my friend said to me, "I don't think God was unhappy we tried. I don't think God was unhappy we stopped. Good things happened. We learned some things. The kingdom wasn't damaged." He was right. But Steve was still furious.

I've known plenty of Steves in my life. The Steves of the world need a plumbline like this one. If they don't agree, they don't belong there. Simple.

My quirks:

I value your opinion, but in what other company would you be able to question your boss at every angle? Ministry does not entitle you to a gripe session with every new endeavor.

Some things need to die. I don't mind killing them. Sometimes, I take joy in killing them.

Staff members must refrain from using the word "purpose." It is banned.

I am involved in a lot of "things." Some wouldn't call them gospel-centric. But I believe the gospel is what happens on the way to the "thing" and in the middle of the "thing" when the Holy Spirit is invited to come along and relationships are invested in. The "thing" doesn't matter.

I don't introduce most of the popular worship songs I hear to the church. I prefer indigenous music and developing songwriters.

Plumbline #7: The Fast Eat the Slow

Leadership is about stewarding energy and momentum. The best way to do that is to seize opportunities as they appear, because quick turnaround tends to build momentum. We want to be able to respond quickly to the Spirit, or to a need, or to our intuition, and that requires us to be constantly in prayer. We pray in advance of any crisis or opportunity so we don't have to slow down and try to hear from God in order to move forward. That way, when good opportunities come, we can capitalize on them quickly and with confidence.

We will debunk the myth that creative collaboration and diversity of opinion is the way to get the best results. We think this is a lie and cause for unnecessary frustration in teams. Things get done when like-minded people seize the moment.

We covered this a bit in Chapter One when I made the statement "Creative collaboration is dumb." By now, you know that a bold and silly statement like this is one of my quirks. I stated the quirk plainly for you in Chapter One before I even defined the path of discovery we are on. I wanted it to shock you the first time you heard it. Because that's how our staff people view some of our quirks. Shocking. Abrasive. Unfair.

Even though I don't always say things so plainly and honestly, my staff feels them. My staff knows when I think things are dumb. So does yours. Your face, impatience, indifference, sarcasm, and joking give you away. This is why it's important to take your quirks to the next level and communicate the greater principle behind your idiosyncrasies.

Publishing your plumblines will do one of two things: it will alienate and divide your staff, or it will get everyone on the same team because they now see inside your head. It may do both. But you need unity. Not necessarily agreement. But unity.

An understanding of the *rules of the road*. Even if it drives some away, this will only be better in the end. Like-minded teams move forward.

More of my quirks:

I don't begin and end every meeting in prayer.

I hate the word "process."

I think "prayerfully considering" something is what most people say they will do to end a conversation and a proposition they don't want to say "no" to right away.

I say no a lot. But I say yes way more.

I don't care if you fail. We'll survive. Unless you aren't trying. Then I care a lot.

Plumbline #8: Bad Behavior Must Be Challenged

When people step out of line, we can't ignore their disrespect. If it is left unchallenged, we will subtly be suggesting to the church that this kind of behavior is acceptable. Leaders need guts to confront good people who sometimes act badly (even if this kind of bad behavior is only as "harmless" as playing the victim). Leaders also need strong spines to confront mean-spirited and malicious folk who seek to forward their own agendas within the church. Of course, the way we challenge bad behavior should be loving and done in the motivation of healthy change and restoration.

My friend and pastor, Ed, died of cancer a while back. I sat under his leadership from the time I was seventeen until my mid-twenties. Before he left this earth, he taught me many valuable things about pastoring. It was during one of his sermons in my early twenties when the Lord encouraged me to go back to school and pursue a Bible and theology education. I watched every move he made with awe and respect. I always found him approachable and interested in me. But not everyone felt this way about Ed.

Some were afraid of him. Some thought he should be more inclusive of others' ideas. Some found him too opinionated. The elders were always at war with him. The old-timers had a hard time adjusting to him when he first came to the church. The old guard didn't trust him. Some tried to start a coup d'état.

I never felt any of those strange things about Ed. I could barely understand where some people misunderstood him. As a young man, I found his leadership so inspiring. It took me years to figure out why some people didn't like Ed.

He had spiritual balls.

Some people weren't used to that.

Some people want their pastors pliable, so they can shape them into their own image.

It was a summer Sunday in 1987. I went to lead music for the high school group as a volunteer for one hour before heading to what we called "big people church." When I walked down the hall to attend the service, I heard a bit of a kerfuffle with the ushers.

On the cover of the Sunday bulletin, where they usually printed scripture and some sort of a welcome greeting, there was a photocopied letter someone had scribbled on the back of a receipt that read something like this:

> *You have nothing wrong with you!*
> *I watched you walk into church*
> *after you parked in this handicap spot!*
> *You should be ashamed of yourself.*

Apparently, someone watched a woman park in a handicap spot and walk into church. When the person spying on this unsuspecting soul determined she shouldn't be parking there because she was able to walk (as if that is the only qualifier for needing a handicap placard), the person decided to become the

Vigilante of Indiscretionary Parking (VIP) and shame this woman by leaving an anonymous note on her windshield.

When this poor woman (who was suffering from a severe heart condition that required keeping her walking to a minimum) got to her car after church let out, she found the note. Unsigned. Just mean. Judgmental. Nasty.

Ed saw her crying in the parking lot. He learned what had happened and decided to make it the topic of his message the following week. He photocopied the nasty note on the cover of the bulletin for all to see. When he got up to speak, the first thing he said was, "Who is ready to own up to this?" He told this poor woman's story of the battle she was fighting. He talked about conflict resolution. He encouraged all to make their peace with the people they cast judgment on. He encouraged all who were bitter toward another to get up from their seats and go to a phone to call those people (this was before the days of cell phones).

It was an incredible day of restoration for many. And the VIP decided to come forward after the message and apologize to the lady. The VIP had a sensitivity to people taking advantage of folks, because his father was in a wheelchair.

Ed called it out. He did what some leaders are not willing to do. Most would have comforted the offended for sure but wouldn't have thought creatively about how to seek out the offender. Most would not have turned the scene into a teaching opportunity for the whole church. Many didn't agree with Ed's modus operandi. Most won't agree with half the things you do as a leader when you challenge bad behavior. No one wants to experience conflict. Not many really want to change.

What would you have done? How would you have remedied the situation and engaged all parties? Is this a leadership principle for you? Think through your quirks. Here are some of mine:

If you tell me, "I talked to a few people who disagree," I will ask you to produce those people before we talk any further. I will not face your invisible army to defend my decision.

Asking a constant complainer and dissenter to leave the church is a viable option for me. I've done it before. I'd do it again.

If an unsigned complaint card comes into our office, the assistants are instructed to throw them away without passing the complaint on to us.

Plumbline #9: We Make Exceptions

We hold our rules loosely, knowing that there may be extenuating circumstances that cause us to reevaluate from time to time. We may also choose to bend/break our own rules based on what God is saying to us through prayer, season, wisdom, and/or consideration.

It's important to mention that while it is necessary to solidify what you already believe about leadership, mission, church, and ministry, it is also important to realize the bride is a living thing. You aren't making rules for a game when you determine what leadership principles you believe. You're creating a roadmap and promoting understanding.

Situations will present themselves in which you may find it wise to bend your own rules. This is part of good leadership as well—being able to read the signs and interpret your own rules in light of circumstances you didn't count on or didn't foresee. When you are leading people, it's important to remember they are just that—people. In church leadership, you will at one time or another make an adjustment in order to prioritize relationship. If you don't have relationships, you don't really have a church.

Our building is not available for weddings and funerals. We don't have the staff to handle it. Our auditorium changes constantly, and the public never knows what they're gonna get. We can't make aesthetic promises, and the auditorium arrangement usually isn't conducive to quick switches. So I put the kibosh on marrying and burying in our space.

But what do you do when one of your greatest volunteers decides to get married and begs to have the wedding in the space where she has given hundreds of hours of her time and calls it home? What do you do when a staff member dies and the family wants the funeral at the church? The answer to both of these for us is, "Duh. We'll do it!" Sometimes we break our own rules because it seems best for everyone involved.

We have a "rule" that no handwritten signs are to be made and placed around the church. But what do you do when you have a professional calligrapher offer to make some signs for an upcoming event? It could be a great opportunity to work with someone, and artistic calligraphy was not the reason we made the rule in the first place. We made the rule for the signs being made with crayon, stained with a coffee cup ring, and duct-taped to the wall.

Here is a word of advice. Please take this to heart. Write it down. Ready? Break your own rules from time to time. You don't have to feel bad about breaking your rules, and you don't have to explain yourself to everyone, but it is wise to have an answer for your exception. You will most likely need to have that answer ready the next time you tell someone no.

Quirks:

If I am able, I will bleed a little more, work a little harder, and sweat more profusely to foster relationship for the sake of the kingdom even if I have to break a rule to do it.

I don't feel bad saying no to someone if it means saying yes to someone else. However, if I can be part of a solution that benefits everyone, I will try to do so.

I don't care if people get mad at me for breaking my own rules even if they will never understand why.

CELEBRATE IT ALL

The process from story to labels to quirks to plumblines can be a very cathartic experience for you. But the process doesn't end with just getting the ideas out of your head. You have to get the ideas into the heads of others. Those ideas have to become part of the thinking process of others. Your plumblines need to become a *staff infection*. Sorry, I couldn't help myself.

For this process to be helpful and feel like a win for everyone, you need to be able to celebrate the process. Plumblines shouldn't feel like rules. Sure, there are a ton of rules you already have and will make up along the way. But plumblines should feel like freedom for everyone. Don't think of these leadership principles as rules, and don't let your staff think of them that way. Think of these principles as your leadership worldview.

Plumblines are the things that will unify your staff. They will be the hub of conversation when it comes to conflict resolution. They will help your staff know how to tailor their ministry endeavors in line with the church's mission and personality. They will save your staff embarrassment. They will put the staff at ease knowing they don't have to guess what's inside your head.

The staff is the most important place to celebrate these principles once you've defined them. The next important place is most likely with your elder team. Let them know how you do business. The next important group of people who need to know your plumblines are your volunteers—especially if those volunteers are being given freedom to craft things and dream things with a good dose of permission and little supervision. The better job you do at communicating and celebrating with your staff, the easier it is for these leadership principles to leak into your congregation and become part of the church's makeup.

From story to celebration, this process of defining what you believe at your core about leadership is an ongoing exercise. Once you feel good about what you've discovered in this process, celebration becomes an ongoing dealio.

TELL ME SOMETHING I DON'T ALREADY KNOW

I'm a fan of learning. And growing. And stretching.

We can always learn new insights from people, books, situations, and passing through conflict. Part of maturity is having an understanding that we don't know everything. I get it.

Too often, however, leaders are afraid to move forward with ideas and initiatives, and they operate with too much caution because they are afraid of the unknown. They are hesitant to make the tough calls until they feel like they have all the information. They are anxious of challenges and being challenged by others, so they avoid change. They are apprehensive about having egg on their face when things don't work out as they planned, so they put on a smiley face and ignore the pressing need for revolution.

Sure, leaders don't know everything. But I'm convinced leaders in any area who take the pulse of the world around them and are willing to bleed for their people have everything they need to know to move forward. The greatest presidents, teachers, community leaders, religious icons, and change agents are remembered most for their selfless attention to the world and people around them.

We're told there are somewhere between seven habits and twenty-one irrefutable laws of effective leadership. I don't deny these are helpful things to know. But I think being a good leader is even easier than that. Most of what you need to know is already in your noggin. You learned it as a child and continue to re-learn it as an adult. It's the stuff we tell our kids when they are running around the neighborhood with friends or going to school:

1. Know who you are and be confident.

2. Play nice.

3. Don't be a jerk.

Augustine said (and is often misquoted), "Love, and do what thou wilt." Sometimes people like to throw "God" in after love when quoting him, but the point is the same. As a quirky leader, I am convinced God is not concerned about what you do as much as He is concerned that you do something.

If you are a quirky leader who is invested in the place you live and the people with whom you live, God has put more capacity and insight inside of you than all the world's leadership books have combined. He has given you a mission specific to the place you live and the people you lead. Love Him. Love others. You know what to do. Do something.

CHAPTER FOUR: ✗ HOOOOO ARE YOU?

When I first arrived at Westwinds, many on staff had forgotten why they existed. Because of the intense conflict the church was in the middle of, the innovative missional groundwork that had been laid was cluttered up. The staff had become like the time of the Judges when "everyone did what was right in his own eyes."

In the absence of someone pointing the way and rallying the troops, the staff members were making decisions about how they used their time and spent their resources based upon how they felt at the time. Because many were sore, angry, depressed, and feeling a bit rebellious, the mission drift of the church was intense. It was as if we dropped off a bunch of teenagers at the missional mall and gave them mad money for retail therapy.

In many ways, there was a missional mutiny. Even people who should have known better had a new battle cry ringing out to the tune of their own disharmonic preference. In the absence of someone talking about mission and why we do what we do in the way we do it, people looked for an opportunity to make their voices heard. Choirs can't have that many soloists.

All of a sudden, a church with a staff that had been somewhat of a flagship ministry, modeling creative interaction with the world around them and innovative missional endeavors, became very interested in its own reflection.

There were arguments about the kind of music we played, the volume of that music, and the places where it was acceptable to play music in town. There were arguments over the "correct style" of preaching. There were arguments over children's ministry programs that were "not doing enough to reach the kids in our own church." There were arguments about what was church appropriate and what was "of the world." A church that once prided itself in going against the grain and not being afraid to fail as it charted new territory became timid, protective, and self-absorbed. That's what churches do when they lose their compass. They hunker down. They bury deep in a foxhole, scream for someone to bring food, and stab one another with bayonets.

There's a reason your church fights about stupid stuff. In the absence of knowing what really matters, individuals will always think about what matters to them (echoes of worship wars rattle in the distance). Church people want the church to be more about what they "like." But Jesus never talked to us about making church pleasant. The mission is to save people and heal the world. When people come to us with petty concerns, it highlights misalignment with mission.

Though our mission statements are usually some version of the Great Commission and might fit on a t-shirt, the process of defining how our mission plays out in everyday decisions and activities is a constant conversation and process. This conversation shouldn't be a task but rather part of the celebration that should become part of who you are.

During this time of rebellion (not everybody was being a punk, just some), it became very clear to me and Randy (before David arrived) that we needed to intervene to get the train back on track. To use a more accurate image, we had to gather the staff members on their Segways and get them heading in the same direction.

To remind the staff and the church what our particular role was as missionaries in our city, we created two new forums for communication and conversation. For the staff, we created what we still refer to as "Sandbox," and for the church at large we created what we called "Loveshack" (now reinvented as "Hivemind"). Before you write these off as clever little naming conventions and part of our funky quirkiness, let me unpack the names for you.

SANDBOX

The thing we wanted more than anything else for our staff members was to learn to play together once again. Learn to share. Learn to party. They were quickly getting to a point where they were combative and protective and had nothing in common. No mission in common. If they were playing at all, they were playing in different corners of the playground.

They all needed a place to gather and play and share their toys. Playing and sharing would come about only if they remembered why ministry was once so fun in the first place. We were willing as leaders to create this central place of play, and we were hopeful that most would want to join in. We knew some would not want to play nice with the others, and we were willing to draw a line in the sand with them.

Sandbox was born.

We took a trip to our local superstore and picked up a dozen sand pails and sand shovels. We put an invitation in every pail to join us at the first meeting of Sandbox the following morning. We set the pails and shovels on every desk in the church workspace.

Of course, everyone hated the idea at first. No one wanted to be forced to play. But through prayer with the help of the Holy Spirit and a relentless desire on our part to bleed for the sake of unity, we all entered the Sandbox. It resembled a tag-team wrestling match before it resembled anything team-like, but we eventually got there.

After a few playtimes, some were asked to leave the Sandbox. Forever. Some found their own way out.

We all got sand in our cracks. Some see sand in their crack as the price you pay to play. Some see sand as an annoyance that isn't worth it. But no play day at the beach happens without a little "How did I get sand *there*?"

When we first started Sandbox, we made some mistakes as leaders. I think in an effort to *set the record straight* and *lay down the law* we overdid it with leader talk. Too many steps to success, too many required reading books on leadership, too many soliloquies and reflections on leadership articles we just read. This didn't feel like playing at all.

Sandbox turned a corner for us when we realized the best way to talk about leadership principles is in the context of mission. And the best way to get everyone to play together and share together was in the context of doing and celebrating the mission.

No one on our staff gave a rat's behind about the *3, 5, or 7 Steps to Whatever* we had to present that day. But when we talked about what our mission was, celebrated what was going on in the church, applauded what results we were seeing in the community, and told stories about the people we were meeting and starting relationships with, it all came together.

We eventually made every fifth Tuesday of the month a time when the whole staff goes offsite and does something fun. Just for the sake of fun. Just to be friends. Inevitably, those times are pregnant with talk about what Jesus is doing in the lives of people in our community.

Sandbox is not a staff meeting. *Staff meeting* has been banned from our lexicon. In our church experience, staff meetings are too often dull, long, one-sided, formal, and a time to check things off a list. They are often a time to chastise. They often happen multiple times a week and feel more like a trip to the principal's office than a celebration. Certainly, we have meetings that are more business-like at the church, but we have those meetings one-on-one when absolutely necessary or we just talk in passing. We don't pull everyone together for time-consuming meetings to hear about things that concern only 25% of them at any one time. Hey, kids! Have you heard of this new communication tool called email?

Sandbox is for playing. For praying. For sharing. For celebrating. For telling stories. For encouraging. For talking about the mission.

LOVESHACK/HIVEMIND

For many of the same reasons we came up with the name Sandbox, we came up with the name Loveshack for the church at large. Loveshack, in its first inception, was a big Sandbox. Our people needed to learn how to love one another. Express love to one another. Say loving things out loud. Get along.

We could think of no better way to express what we wanted to happen in a corporate meeting environment where we celebrated mission than to name that gathering after an '80s hit by the B-52s that described a place in the woods where people all gathered to have casual sexual encounters. Ahem, that was a joke. Actually, we never really thought too deeply about the connections some might make with that title, and it's one of the reasons we eventually changed the name to Hivemind.

Hivemind seemed a more fitting name anyway. We want our people to work toward acting and thinking in unison around the mission. We want them on the same page. We want individual ideas to emerge in the context of "we're all in this together," as opposed to one salmon swimming downstream in the missional river.

We have changed the format of this gathering many times over. When it starts to become predictable, we give it a kick in the rear and jumpstart it once again. The format isn't what's important. It's about the getting together.

At times, Hivemind has seemed more business-like. And, at other times, it has felt like a circus. We have a conviction that every church needs to get together and hang. When you are living missionally, you have many stories to share and celebrate. Those stories become the outline of your hang-time. Over a meal. By candlelight. In a secret surprise setting. In the round. In small groups. By the bonfire. It doesn't matter. It just matters that you have an opportunity to gather and celebrate the mission.

While everyone at the church is invited to Hivemind, it is a requirement for our *Owners*.

OWNERSHIP

When I was young in ministry, I asked a pastor friend about the membership process at his church. "We don't have membership, dude." (He pastored at a Southern California Calvary Chapel.) "Jesus' church is for everyone. It's not about jumping through hoops."

For years, I bought that. I get it. I understand why some churches don't have membership requirements. Maybe you feel the same as I have toward membership.

- Membership leaves some people feeling like they are on the outside.

- Membership seems like requiring something extra to be part of the church when Jesus simply says, "Come unto me."

- Membership sounds a lot like privilege.

While we weren't huge fans of many of the models we had seen for membership, we had some communication issues in the church and a mission misalignment that needed addressing, and it seemed to us some kind of process akin to membership could help.

Ownership was designed in a way that addresses the pitfalls of church membership right at the start. It is a process that allows us to get to know individuals and talk about what we do and why we do it the way we do it. The process allows us to uncover any vision differences with individuals and develop camaraderie. Ownership is an opportunity for us and any other leaders to talk about what we believe about mission in the place where we live.

If you were to start the process of becoming an Owner at Westwinds, we would tell you *Ownership is not about privilege*. It is about giving up your rights. It's about parking next door to free up spaces in our parking lot. It's about serving. It's about making yourself available to others. It does not give you a vote. It's about being the person God has made you to be in the community you live. You can't separate who you are from where you live in God's economy.

The process of *Ownership* is as simple as a conversation. We have a printed *Ownership Manual* that outlines everything we believe theologically, methodologically, systematically, missionally, and every other "_____-ally" we could think of. When the time is right for individuals, they set an appointment with a pastor or elder to go through the manual. This is done in a casual setting. At the end of that meeting, if all is understood and everyone is on the same page, both parties sign the manual.

That's it.

Whether you believe in a process or gatherings like this or not, I'm sure you are aware that you cannot over-communicate as a leader. You will sometimes feel like you have said something one thousand times when, in reality, you probably said it only a handful of times and thought about it the other few hundred. And, as many times as you have communicated your thoughts out loud, chances are people heard it only once. If you're lucky.

So how does a leader with quirks that make it glaringly obvious he or she has very specific ideas about mission bring people along for the ride? If you have a communication system that makes mission a conversation and everyone is on the same page, please share your secret with us. For most of us, mission alignment and mutual missional understanding is an ongoing battle. I haven't met anyone who has cracked the code—not even my pastor friends who have house churches of 12 people.

If your church is doing anything worthwhile, if you are making dents in breaking down walls in your community, if you are pushing the boundaries of what it means to be a missional community, there are people who exist in your church who still don't know what is inside your head. They are craving more info. As leaders, we sometimes get very frustrated with these folks. We feel like we have beaten the mission horse to death, or at least faint breaths. If one more person asks why we do XYZ, we might explode. Or implode.

But is it really their fault for not knowing the mission? Sometimes, yes. But not always. If there is an epidemic of missional question askers in your church, it may be that at least part of the problem lies with us as leaders. I know. I know. It's hard to remember they aren't your enemy. They don't all mean to be buggy (only some do). Many want to be on your side.

I am horrible at this. I am preaching to myself when I say these words. I have that disease where everything is so clear in my head in regard to the direction we are headed that I am absolutely amazed my brain hasn't leaked on to you. This is why we created Sandbox. And Hivemind. And Ownership. And we still have holes.

We can't always communicate on a Sunday morning the plethora of information we want our committed folks to know. For us, *Ownership* provides another opportunity to communicate mission alongside *Sandbox, Hivemind,* and other special occasions and vehicles.

We need to provide feedforward to our people—let people know what is happening in advance—especially regarding important issues, initiatives, and potentially controversial message series or missional endeavors. We want to answer objections before they come.

We want to know who is on our team, and we want them to know the others on the team. It's good to know who is in your corner. *Ownership* provides opportunities to become better acquainted with these folks. Do you know who to go to when the big proverbial fan is ready to receive the big proverbial doody? You want to identify these people. When someone wants to thwart the mission or poke holes in it, you don't want to be the only one speaking up. When you speak out against naysayers, you sound defensive. When the community lives in such a way that silences the naysayers, you're off the hook, and the issues tend to go away.

You want input. Right? Not suggestions. Not a complaint box. You want the people who are deeply committed and elbows deep in the mission to be able to speak into what is and isn't successful or aligned with mission. It is impossible (and not wise) to listen to every kind of input. Everyone has an opinion, and many conflict. For us, *Ownership* allows us to recognize the people who are committed to the mission and not fear their input and questions as divisive but rather see them in light of the mission from a spirit with a pure motive. How do you create an atmosphere where people feel welcome and encouraged to give input?

MISSIONAL PLUMBLINES

Most churches have a mission statement that is a form of the Great Commission. But no matter how cleverly we talk about going out into the world and making disciples, most people don't know what *you* mean when you say it.

When Mike made plans to visit his friends' church, he couldn't wait to see all the wonderful things they were doing in the community. Mike had heard so much about their creativity and innovation. He heard they were meeting needs of their community in ways that no other organization had. He had just moved into town and went to church that day with great expectations. But Mike was very disappointed in what he experienced when he finally arrived.

First, he hated the music. Not that it was played poorly; it just wasn't his style. The church had a very heavy country music vibe, and it didn't float Mike's boat.

Second, the church was doing nothing to feed the poor in the community as far as he could see. Mike came from an inner-city church that had a soup kitchen every Tuesday and Thursday, but all he saw in his friends' church was a cafeteria-sized lobby and a kitchen that barely got used.

The nail in the coffin for Mike was the fact that they had no Sunday School program. Mike grew up in a church that provided Christian education classes every Sunday where folks could learn about everything from Genesis through Revelation.

John was new to church. He had attended the local Bible church as a kid but didn't have anything to show for that experience except the scars of guilt lashings. Now, in his forties, he walked into the same church Mike did and found something completely different.

He found a church that played the kind of music he and all his friends were listening to. Stylistically, it felt right. Sometimes they even did covers of some of his favorite artists. They had a lot of variety, and he couldn't believe how much different the music was from the church experience he had had as a kid.

John rode his Harley to church his first Sunday. He wanted to make a statement. He figured he would wear all his rebel colors just to see if anyone cared. They didn't. As a matter of fact, they embraced him in the lobby and talked about how "sweet" his "ride" was. One of the ushers happened to lead a satellite affinity group at the church dedicated to bikers. John was pleasantly surprised.

John entered the sanctuary and was enthralled with the eye candy. Obviously, this place was full of artists. It was anything but sterile and a stark contrast to the cafeteria-like sanctuary he once visited.

Margaret attends the same church Mike and John visited. She didn't get a chance to meet either one of them. She loves her church, serves there on the coffee team, and gives regularly. She is new to Christianity and church and used to feel like the church could do no wrong. Until that one Sunday.

Margaret found out the church was part of a fundraiser project at the local pub. A bunch of musicians and artists from the church were planning on playing music there and selling paintings. The money was going to a local charity for struggling families.

Margaret had no problem with the idea of giving money away. She had a huge problem with the way they were going about it. Margaret fell in love with Jesus through her involvement in Alcoholics Anonymous. As a recovering alcoholic, Margaret has a firm belief that Jesus and booze don't mix. Margaret believes Jesus saved her *from* the booze. She was beyond baffled at the choice of one of the pastors to be involved with this "so-called ministry."

Steve is what some might call a *founding member* of the same church. He has stories about how they used to meet in someone's apartment and how, twenty years later, they now have a beautiful building and are a known entity in the community.

Steve is one of the biggest givers to the church. Always has been. His kids grew up there. They started attending right after his divorce twenty years ago. Back then, he was far from what he would call the "Jesus-y type." He was a womanizer, a cocaine addict, and one of the wealthiest businessmen in town, describing himself as a "self-made man." He didn't feel like he needed Jesus until the Holy Spirit and loving friends broke through to him. He loves to tell his story.

But one day Steve got extremely angry. He heard the new youth center the church had built was designating an area outside the building for kids who smoke. He had a suspicion that the new youth pastor was not focusing on kids who were part of church families. He heard the new pastor "had a heart for fringe kids." This smoking section proved his suspicions true.

Steve wrote a letter to the senior pastor and demanded the new youth pastor be put on probation, or he would stop tithing. His letter was full of harsh accusations and Bible verses.

Most likely, your church has Mikes, Johns, Margarets, and Steves. They all go to my church too. People with an outside-in view and an idea of what that church should be doing in their community. People who are genuinely surprised at how awesome church can be and wish it had been different for them growing up. People who once felt the church was perfect and then had their world rocked by some decision that didn't line up with their idea of what church should be. People who have forgotten where they came from, who need reminders about why the church exists in the first place.

They all exist in the same church culture where the same things are communicated time and time again. They hear the same messages on Sundays. They get the same emails. They read the same bulletins. They are invited to the same informational meetings and vision-casting sessions.

They all think they understand the mission. But mission plays out in quirky ways some times. It's not always easy for people to connect the dots. We can't over-communicate the reasons why we choose to support missional endeavors. For some communities, mission may look like partnering with a local pub. Or a nursing home. Or a school. It may mean all those things and more. But not everyone sees the *why* as clearly as those leading the endeavor do. And, as frustrating as it can be, we sometimes have some 'splaining to do.

If it sounds like I'm talking out both sides of my mouth, I am.

Leaders should feel no shame in having a compelling and specific direction without having to explain themselves at every turn. But, at the same time, if we want people to come alongside us, we need to give feedforward. Some will never understand the why. Some will disagree even when they do understand. We can't change that. But we can work harder at making sure more people do understand, support, cheerlead, and become proactive about the mission.

I don't think I have a corner on this market. One of my fears in writing this book is that you will come away with some idea that I have all this locked down. Far from it. Here's a secret (with only a tiny bit of hyperbole): every preacher's best sermons come from a place deep inside where he or she struggles with the very things being preached against. Not every preacher gives that self-disclosure, but it's true most of the time. I promise.

I often get frustrated with some people's lack of understanding when it comes to missional endeavors—the things we do *out there*. I get impatient sometimes when I have to explain something to someone who should know better. I have an allergic reaction to those who try to steer mission into safe and pleasant risk-free territory.

But it's hard to know where people are on the continuum of missional understanding according to your church's personality and your quirks. Some opinions don't count. Some should weigh heavily. Some are in learning mode. Some will never learn. Some desperately want to understand. Some want to tell you how wrong you are. The only way you can differentiate is to spell out the quirky ways you believe God has called you to be missional in your community.

Just like you discovered your leadership quirks and plumblines through observation and interpretation in light of your story and your labels, you need to discover and publish your missional plumblines. Here are some of our missional plumblines.

Plumbline #10 Everybody Matters

Because everybody matters both to God and to us, those ministries that reach more people will be better resourced. Resources, after all, are almost always limited and should be allocated to those ministries that produce results. We cannot be afraid to discontinue ministries that produce very limited results, if for no other reason than that they draw on the time and energy and availability of our staff (who could be better utilized once freed from these low-return responsibilities).

A long time ago, we discontinued a program designed for children. It was a weekly evening program that ran much like the Cub Scouts. It included Bible memorization, games, and some worthwhile exercises for kids. But only church kids came to it. That didn't make it bad, but it certainly didn't make it missional.

Those who ran it promised it had potential to bring in kids from the community. In an effort to do so, they changed the name and took out some of the *churchy* structure and language. They started with great gusto. Fell back into the old routine. Got tired. Numbers dwindled.

We cancelled it.

Some left the church. In fact, two of the four families the program mattered to left the church.

We were sad to lose them for sure, but we could not justify the cost of keeping this flailing ministry around. It cost money. Time. Effort. Energy. Staff help. Volunteers. Building maintenance. Advertising.

For four families.

Here's another story . . .

One of the Owners of our church came to us and expressed a desire to install heating systems in the homes of some people in the community who didn't have central heating systems. He told us of many families he knew of in the area that didn't even have wood or gas fireplaces. Their old homes had failed systems from yesteryear, and they kept warm with blankets and space heaters.

On his own, he made a partnership with local HVAC companies to provide free labor for installations. He put together a team of people who cared for families who were going to be recipients, tore out their old systems, and made way for the new. He generated excitement in our community, and we raised extra funds on top of some missional money we had set aside for great ideas like this.

During one of the coldest winters in the last ten years, multiple families got HVAC systems installed in their homes. We asked for nothing in return. Many shared their stories with us on video. Some made our church their home. We made many friends. Jesus' name was lifted high. The whole church became part of the celebration. The local media covered stories surrounding the effort.

That year, we spent the same amount of money and WAY less effort giving families free heat than we would have spent on the fledgling club for four families.

Here are some of our quirks behind this plumbline:

We will never entertain a conversation in which we continue doing something because it's always been done.

Ministries within the church, large or small, do not get money simply because they have a name and exist.

We may encourage you to try your idea without any financial help from the church. It doesn't mean we don't think it's worthwhile, but we need to calculate potential results and reach.

We don't think the argument "if just one person comes to Jesus it's all worth it" is a valid guiding principle for a plan of execution.

Plumbline #11 We Are Missionaries to Our Culture

The dominant cultural figure in America today is the post-Christian, media-driven consumer. Typically, Americans value their anonymity in religious and spiritual contexts. They care about how things are labeled (or even whether they're labeled at all, which is why we have an aversion to "church-y" language), because naming conventions matter.

Our task is to bring the gospel into this culture in much the same way as the great missionaries of the past brought the gospel all over the world. We must help the people of our world understand the gospel by placing the message of Christ in terms they can understand. To that end, the first thing we must do is exegete the culture. We have to figure out the world around us as the culture understands it, not as we wish it would be. This requires us to stay in step with the culture (i.e., to be early adopters), using music and art and aesthetics and references that [1] abide by their own rules and [2] are representative of the times and of the people.

Quite a few years ago, I had a group of people try to recruit me to play in their Christian music festival in town. They had recruited many bands from the area to play in a local park. They told me it was an outreach event. The cost was only $10.00 a person. Many churches were represented in the lineup of musicians. Some of the bands were not "phenomenal musicians," but they had "great hearts" and a "sound message." The festival would have "praise-drumming circles." There would be jam sessions of "spontaneous praise." The concert was going to be called something along the lines of "Praiseapalooza."

I declined.

My quirks:

I distrust events that are clearly inwardly centered and for the church but are labeled as outreach events.

Just because music has lyrics that speak about God doesn't make it beautiful or skillful or good.

I don't like overused naming conventions like everything-palooza. And when those naming conventions are attached to church events, it sounds kind of cheesy and uncreative to me. I feel the same way about branding church events by stealing the styling of another popular brand, such as taking a Disney logo and turning it in to a church kids program logo.

But, most of all, in light of this event . . .

I have limited missional hours to spend. I want them to count. When I get together with a bunch of other Christians to sing, it may be worthwhile, but it probably has nothing to do with outreach. I have another category of time designated for stuff I do with other Christians.

My friends on the concert committee could not understand how I could turn down their invitation. One gentleman was pretty fired up about it. "I'm so surprised at you. How can you say you have a heart for lost people and turn down such a great opportunity to be a light for Jesus in the community?"

I don't react well to attempts at guilt motivation. This gentleman's comment to me questioned my motivation, character, and heart for people by suggesting I should feel bad. As if everyone but me could clearly see that participating was the right decision. It was the equivalent of getting a picture of a weeping Jesus on Facebook telling me that if I didn't forward the picture to all my friends, I was letting the devil win. (This actually has happened to me as well. Many times over. Sometimes the picture is of starving kids, Jesus holding a lamb, rainbows, or kittens.)

I had lunch with this gentleman to help him see inside my head. I explained to him that my decision to decline had nothing to do with *his* heart or motivation. I told him we had different ideas of what mission looks like. I spent this time with him because we have a bit of a relationship and history that dictated further conversation.

He prodded me and told me I was closed-minded. He told me to get off my high horse. He told me I thought my music was better than his. He told me I was limiting God and God could use anything he wanted to draw people to himself.

I agree about the last part. God speaks through anything he wants. He's used talking jackasses before. Doesn't mean he prefers it. Doesn't mean we can be one.

I will never see eye to eye with this gentleman about his concert. He asked me to join Praiseapalooza 2 the following year. With the other twelve people who actually showed up.

I wish I could go back to that conversation. I believe at this point in my ministry experience, after having identified my quirks more clearly and developing plumblines that are more potently stated, I could do a better job talking through why I declined.

Being missionaries to our culture is about being part of a conversation with people who don't know Jesus. All the time. It's about doing life with people who aren't church people. It's about understanding what people are listening to, reading, creating, and watching. It's about listening to their needs. Understanding what compels them and moves them. It's more than presentation. It's not about making people our projects. It's about relationship that says, "I care about you."

A friend of mine who pastors a church across town recently got into a scrap with his elder board over mission. He wanted to discontinue their number one outreach in the church: knocking on doors and handing out Bible tracts.

It's their number one outreach not because it is the most effective thing they do. It's number one because it's the only thing they do. It's not number one because people are becoming followers of Jesus. They aren't. But they've been doing this method of evangelism in their little church for the last hundred years and training people to duplicate this method.

My friend brought these concerns to his board. One elder said, "The next thing you are going to tell us is it's okay to sit at the bar with someone and talk about Jesus." His honest answer got him fired.

Here are two other plumblines of ours that may help you in determining your own in regard to mission:

Plumbline #12 Everything in Submission

The mission is the whole entire reason we have a church in the first place. It's all about the mission. Mission first, mission only. Things that deter us or attempt to co-opt our energies (like political agendas or social agendas) must not be tolerated within the church. The established power brokers cannot have control at the expense of the mission. The newbies cannot wrest control away at the expense of the mission.

We must also be careful that the internal needs and desires of the church don't force us to become insular and unconcerned about the world around us. Outreach should always trump in-reach.

Over the years, we have had people ask to plaster cars with fliers, stake lawn signs on our property in support of ballot measures, or put posters in our lobby drawing attention to *issues*. We say no to all of them. Because Jesus is the *issue* we want to herald. Period. As such, some have left the church saying we don't care about them. This is not true at all. We care deeply about them. About them falling in love with Jesus. About them being on his team. That's the one that counts.

Too many times, the noise of other messages crowds out the mission. It's not that those things are necessarily competing messages in and of themselves or that they don't matter at all; it's that they matter much less. The sum of many lesser things in unison is often derailing.

Plumbline #13 Relationships Are Formed "On Mission"

Relationships are not an end unto themselves, but they occur along the way. Groups that are meant to form relationships often fail to do so because they feel contrived and self-serving. Because of this, purely social events will always be our lowest priority and receive the least amount of resources, if any at all.

It's a tall order to start a small group in your home with a group of strangers and expect everyone to huddle and cuddle immediately. If we were interested in facilitating ways for people to meet other people or hang out, we'd probably start a dance club. It's more fun. And less awkward.

We've had a love-hate relationship with small groups (we call them satellites) for a long time. It's not that they don't work ever, but we often put unfair expectations on them (e.g., everyone will fall in love with each other; everyone will connect through the book we study; friendships will be formed). You can't force relationship into a twelve-week study in someone's living room. And why would you?

We can't build relationships from the outside. We can't make *relationship* a realistic primary goal in any group or endeavor of any size, or we will be disappointed. Putting a priority on *mission* allows for relationships to be formed on the way to something and in the middle of something. Something bigger than ourselves.

WHAT ARE YOUR PEOPLE ALREADY DOING?

One more thing about mission. No one understands mission like the people who are already doing it.

One of the key ingredients of Porn Weekend and the main reason for its successful follow-up and follow-through with hurting folks was the involvement of the people of Westwinds who were already doing recovery ministry in the

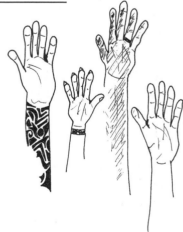

community. We were able to enlist the help of counselors, marriage therapists, addiction specialists, and many people who had successfully put aside a pornography addiction.

Porn Weekend met a need that wasn't being met in the community at large and especially not the church community. There was nothing on a grand scale drawing attention to the problem. However, while we started many satellite support groups that carried on for some time, our biggest success was in getting people connected outside the church in organizations that were better suited to help them.

We don't have an ongoing pornography ministry. We don't feel bad for that. We know where to go for help, and we certainly played a part as a catalyst for drawing attention to a problem no one was talking about.

We learned a valuable insight early on in our shared-leadership ventures: successful leadership in ministry does not necessitate starting new programs. God is active in your people in ways you do not know. God is sometimes more active outside your church than he is within the context of your church. And he is active through your people. Those people are attracted to your church in part because of what they think you believe about mission. If you want some people to light up about mission, empower them and knight them. Recognize what they are doing counts.

When we dreamed up Porn Weekend, it may not have been exactly what some folks in the missional community first envisioned. But it didn't take long to connect the dots when we empowered them to own it, dream alongside us, and, quite frankly, make it more successful than we had imagined, with little *internal* controversy.

Churches are full of people working with organizations outside the church that have spent thousands of dollars to develop programs and an infrastructure to meet specific needs in the community. For example, Lisa works with a para-church ministry dedicated to helping mothers deal with grief and guilt after they have had an abortion. Bethany works with United Way, and they are doing an incredible job of helping people whose homes are about to be foreclosed. Jenny works with a Catholic-funded charity that exists to get people food and clothing.

In many churches, leadership would see Lisa, Bethany, and Jenny as people they could tap in to start new ministries in *their* church. Lisa would become head of some ministry called something like, "Jesus Heals." Bethany would be asked to lead a ministry called something like, "He Did Not Have a Home." And Jenny would be asked to lead some ministry called something like, "Love and Loaves."

Over the years, the bride of Jesus has wasted much time, effort, and money reinventing valuable ministry opportunities in order to sanitize them and give them cute names so they become *church-worthy* ministries. People with great hearts and motives have lost ground by refusing to embrace perfectly legitimate missional endeavors in their community simply because they weren't run by Christian organizations and didn't have Christian naming conventions.

Many years ago, Christian musician Steve Taylor sang about this problem in the church as wanting to drink milk only from a Christian cow. Why are some churches so set on doing things their own way, as opposed to partnering with others who are already meeting that specific need, and sometimes doing a way better job than one church could possibly do starting from scratch? Fear. Control. A misunderstanding about what it means to be in the world and not of the world. Confusion over what it means to be unequally yoked.

Until we learn to play in the same sandbox as not-yet-Jesus-followers, our towns will be full of empty, exclusive sandboxes that no one wants to join. There are signs in too many sandboxes that say "Set Apart" or "Not Good Enough for Jesus." We have many franchises of the church that have become the snobby little rich girl who lets you join her club only if she gets what she wants. The empty sandboxes are not helping us be salt and light in the world. We've created our own worlds. And in these worlds, the salt often has lost its flavor.

Lisa, Bethany, and Jenny are missional powerhouses. They are Jesus to people every day in very tangible ways. When asking yourself, "What do we already believe about mission?" it's important also to ask, "What do our people already believe about mission?" Lisa, Bethany, and Jenny will be thrilled to tell you what they are doing, and they will have many ideas about how the church can come alongside them.

The missional personality of your church is already shaped in many ways by how your people are already spending their time missionally outside your church. If you don't seek to understand this as a leader, there are other potential pitfalls besides wasted energy, time, and resources. There are potential relationship conflicts.

Jan and her husband, Robert bought a second home in their city and dedicated that space to helping children after school. Many kids in their city go home to an empty house every day— empty of family and empty of food. Jan loves the inner-city kids as if they were her own. She feeds them, plays games with them, helps them do homework, braids their hair, and helps them hone their artistic talent. Robert works two jobs. One of his jobs pays for the ability to minister to these neglected children.

A couple of years ago, Jan and Robert approached their church and asked for some financial help. They wanted to put an addition on the home and hire some help, but they were already swimming in debt. The repairs they had done to the home the year before required taking out a loan.

The church responded by telling Jan and Robert they needed to get into a money management program at their church. They told them the church might be willing to help financially after they finished the program, but they would have to be willing to change the name of their home to reflect the church's partnership. Jan and Robert declined the ultimatums. They left the church.

Two months later, the church decided to have an afterschool program in its own building for the kids in the neighborhood. The first week had about thirty kids. Then twenty. By week four, they were down to five kids. In two months, they stopped the program.

The point of this story is not that the church should have joined up with Jan and Robert without any influence or qualifications. Churches are businesses as well, and sometimes it isn't always smart to support an endeavor even if it is a great idea. I know I've given you limited details, but trust me when I say Jan and Robert did not feel *supported*. They felt *accused* and *shamed*. And they felt like the church was more interested in a hostile takeover than a partnership. In this case, they were right.

I'm not suggesting you come alongside every person willy-nilly and support his or her crazy idea to save the world. I'm not saying you should spend money on every good idea your people are a part of. I'm not saying you can't start ministries in your church that are like other ministries in town. I'm not saying your church should be a part of every good thing happening in the community—that's not always practical or smart.

I am saying that for you to lead effectively in the way you are shaped, in the town you are in, with the people you are called to lead, you need to pay attention to what is already happening around you. You need to listen and learn from your people. You need to assess needs in the community at large and ask if God is calling you to lead your church in those directions. Chances are, the people who are attracted to your church and your leadership style are doing the kinds of things in the community that you want to be a part of. Just be aware.

IF YOU CHOOSE TO ACCEPT IT

Every Thanksgiving through Christmas season at our church, we are presented with opportunities to meet needs in the community. There are endless food drives, clothing drives, and fundraisers we are asked to participate in or support. They are all worthy. You can't argue with giving stuff away to people in need.

But we can't do them all. And we shouldn't. If we tried, we would fail. We wouldn't meet others' expectations. We would be spread too thin. People would end up owning initiatives by default and become bitter. It wouldn't be a good use of resources. People would be conflicted about where to give. People would feel guilty about not giving where they aren't able. It would be a mess. We wouldn't have the energy to cheerlead it all. We would end up half-assing most of it and sequestering energy from the things we are zealous about to the detriment of everything and everyone involved.

Not everything that is right for the world is sensible for our community (corporately). The holiday season is a tiny reflection of a grander problem. And a grander opportunity. Identifying what we *cannot* do as a corporate community, and what we don't have the capacity to lead well, enables us to say a *resounding yes* to the things God has birthed in us to rally around and knock out of the ballpark.

When missional opportunities and endeavors arise out of our communities, the individuals leading the charge will want the full support of the White House. They will want to know we, the leadership, are behind them—praying, resourcing, coaching, promoting, and cheerleading. We can be the kind of support they desire only when a rhyming mission has been birthed in us. If we ignore this necessity, we do the mission, the individuals, and ourselves no favors. Everything and everyone suffers.

The way we are missional and want our people to incarnate themselves in our communities is shaped by our own preferences, personalities, demographics, and personal histories, to name a few. To cheerlead mission, identify what mission means in our community, and celebrate missional wins, the church needs to know what mission looks like and what it does not look like.

The only way to get there is by defining what mission *is* and *is not* according to you, the leader.

CHAPTER FIVE :
WILL THE REAL [LEADER'S NAME HERE] PLEASE STAND UP ?

Do you remember when ministry was fun? Do you remember when you got your call? Do you remember the dreams you had about how you and Jesus would be the dynamic duo? Do you remember when a church plant sounded like a great idea because it ended with people actually coming to know Jesus? For many of you, somewhere along the line, ministry beat these things out of you—not the ministry you love but the ministry you allowed to happen to you.

What you believe about ministry determines how you handle everything. From conflict resolution, sin, and team building to shaping your particular brand of church experience, your ministry philosophy determines how you do life inside the church. If mission is the stuff we do with and for the people "out there," then ministry is the stuff that happens with the people coming in the doors of our church as well as our philosophy about the look and feel of the things our leadership is willing to stamp our particular church's brand on. These things make or break us.

If the categories of Leadership, Mission, Ministry, and Church get fuzzy for you, it's okay. They do for us too. You may find other categories that work better for you to communicate your plumblines. You may not want to split them into categories at all. You may find your plumblines cross boundaries into other categories and it's hard to differentiate between them. We feel the same way sometimes. The point of plumblines is not necessarily clear organization of the principles as much as it is clear communication of them.

Our category of ". . . Ministry" is not supposed to be esoteric. But we couldn't find a better word to describe these thoughts that infect the way we do life with people and run programs and everything that happens on the way to doing those things.

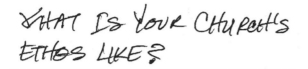

The word *ethos* is one of those words that makes its way into the lunchtime conversation at most church conferences. It's almost as popular as talking about the DNA of your church. While most of us have some general idea about what we mean when we use these words, I take particular issue with the word *ethos*.

Ethos is an Aristotelian word that has more to do with character than personality. Yet, when we talk about a church's ethos, we more often than not are referring to the vibe, feel, and atmosphere of the place and the people. Ethos has become a way to describe the feeling we get when we attend a church or describe a particular experience. This is only partly right.

In public speaking circles, ethos is understood in terms of the believability of the person speaking. Orators have good ethos when they sound like they know what they are talking about and they're smoking what they're selling.

In church settings, ethos should more accurately be thought of as believability. People can smell a fake a mile away. People know when we are putting on a show. People are leery and have grown weary of the church that is Six Flags over Jesus.

Your good ethos quotient is more readily understood over time, but initial impressions of what happens on the weekend and throughout your weekly ministries weighs heavily into the decision people make about whether to believe you're legit and not just trying to sell them some bill of goods.

Your church's ethos will not be judged on the size of its worship rock band. It will however, be judged on the quality and believability of the song choices and people participating in the band no matter what size it is. Your church's ethos will not be judged on the quality of the orator's jokes or hairstyle (unless he or she is obviously trying to be something they are not) but rather on his or her sensitivity, honesty, integrity, self-disclosure, and ability to invite people in to a conversation rather than speak at them. Our lobby may be designed to say "We Care," but if it has trash lying all around, it says something different. We may say "We Value Creativity," but if we repackage the same idea over and over, we negate our own value.

From my experience, I have concluded that of all the areas in which we have quirks, it is our thoughts on *ministry* that will cause us one of the greatest amounts of pain if we do not have well-defined plumblines.

Here are some plumblines that more concisely communicate what we believe about ministry:

Plumbline #14 Christian Spirituality Is about Transformation

At Westwinds, we say "come dirty," but the clear implication is "get clean." It is only through the power of the Spirit that we are changed; our own efforts will always fall short. Therefore, the transformational ethic is embodied in Spirit-centered living. We are meant to stay in step with the Spirit, respond to him, and be changed.

We want to be "editable" (by the Spirit, by others, by scripture, by prayer, by conscience). This transformation happens progressively, which means that every single person is somewhere on a kind of holy continuum on his or her spiritual journey. It also means that the people we're looking for to help us fulfill the mission of the church are often right under our nose—they just need to be developed and discipled.

Bill is an older gentleman at our church. He has been a Jesus follower for only a few short years. Some might call him *rough around the edges*. He has had more than fifty years of practice to make him that way.

On one particular Sunday when I was speaking, I saw Bill in the wings as if he were waiting to talk to me after The Cue (our weekly gathering) was over. He was very patient as I talked with ten or so others before him. He looked angry with me as he made a beeline for me, his eyes burning with intention.

"Thank you," he said. "That was one of the best f#@k!ng sermons I've ever heard. I will take that to heart."

Yes, I was surprised. But it was the physical context (church building) and the occasion (the sermon) that made his expletive startling. I wouldn't have flinched had I heard the word while walking around town. I wouldn't have scolded a teenager at the mall. So what should my response to Bill have been? I can tell you what it was: "Thank you." Then I asked Bill to go to lunch with me to get to know him better.

Plumbline #15 We Are Not the Sin Police

Spirituality isn't about behavior modification so much as it is about transformation and renewal through the power of the Spirit. We don't want to focus all our energy on people's failings, shortcomings, guilt, and woe. We don't ignore sin, but choose instead to focus all our energy on the good news of the gospel because our goal isn't merely correction, but re-orientation.

I don't know about your church, but ours is full of sinners *wink.*

We have found, however, that by spending our energy and attention on the person of Jesus Christ, people get convicted on their own without our help. Or, better yet, the Holy Spirit does his work. This doesn't mean we ignore wrongdoing. The Bible gives us instruction on how we go about correcting and reproving people in our care. But all that instruction is in the context of relationship. It is not our place to point out sin randomly to folks with whom we are not in relationship.

Our owners and team leaders understand that there is a greater scrutiny that comes with responsibility. Within relationship, we encourage loving correction, conflict management, confession, and help on the path to restoration.

Sometimes people ask us to preach on specific *sins*. Sometimes people ask us to call out specific sins of people in the church. Sometimes parents ask us to discipline their children by sitting them down and pointing out their sin. Sometimes spouses ask if we will take their husbands or wives out and talk to them about what they are doing wrong.

We prefer to spend our time by helping people get reoriented and focused on Jesus. We don't believe change happens from the outside in. Rather, the opposite. Imposing a bunch of rules on people has never worked to change a heart. Just ask anyone who wandered around the desert for forty years with Moses. They'll have a few stories for you.

Plumbline #16 Everything Should Be Done with Excellence and Care

We work toward version 4 of every idea (an initial concept, plus three rounds of revision). Everything is subject to peer review. Every first draft gets pushback. We don't like things that look like they didn't take too long. This is why we steer away from things like clip art, crafts and craft-y things, clutter, homemade fliers, crayons and markers on posters, etc. Excuses are not acceptable here, though people will often try to make them.

I have very strong opinions about things of aesthetic value at the church. From time to time, I need to bend my own rules and make allowances for things I don't find particularly of the A+ variety. But, because I believe opinions count and people form theirs partly on the aesthetic, I guard this plumbline closely.

This can be very difficult at times. I have hurt feelings trying to be a gatekeeper here. I believe in it, but I haven't always done a great job in the execution. I have learned it is way easier to communicate expectations beforehand, especially when it comes to the creative process. But, sometimes, someone still ends up getting hurt.

People around our church have been aware of our quirks in this arena for a long time.

We don't allow events where we use plastic tablecloths, plastic forks, and paper plates.

We don't allow posters made with markers to be taped to the walls.

We don't like cheap, mismatched furniture to be used in the church building.

We don't like clip art and emoticons decorating church newsletters.

Because of these quirks and a standard we have set for excellence, people often come in to our building and are immediately wowed by the art, detail, and thought that goes into creating a beautiful space.

Admittedly, some of the choices we make are subjective. Such is art. But someone has to guide and protect branding. David and I are those people. Outside of branding, David and I have a high regard for beauty, and we believe it is partly our responsibility to create a space and experience that reflects that beauty because we see it as a signpost to God.

For years, we believed that while opinions on what is beautiful certainly vary, there is most definitely a standard we can all agree on when it comes to what is unsightly. We could have not been more wrong.

Most people in your church have no well-formed theology of beauty. In the battle of form vs. function, many will allow function to win every time. This is why some churches look like majestic cathedrals and some look like Costco. We have very specific opinions about form and function (which I made obvious by my reference to churches that look like Costco).

Tina was organizing an event for the church at the request of one of the pastors. Her willingness to help was certainly valued. She was given a budget for promotion, a graphic artist who was willing to help in any way, a list of volunteers who were willing to help, a list of expectations for the job, and clear direction (this is what the pastor believed, anyway).

She was stellar in so many ways. Except when it came to promotion.

When the day came to hang posters around the church promoting the event, her pastor was not happy. All of the posters for the church's 20ᵗʰ Anniversary Celebration were made with a Sharpie pen and poster board. Poorly. While Tina's initial enthusiasm said, "I will make this my own!" her posters said, "I am a busy mom who just wants to check this off my list." In fact, that was exactly the case.

Without shaming (as best he could), the pastor had a hard talk with her. He didn't want to devalue the effort she made in so many other areas. But the posters were unacceptable. Tina did not respond well. She got angry at the pastor and screamed, "No one cares about that crap. They just want the information." After a long talk, she reluctantly conceded and had posters made by the in-house designer.

During the next couple of months, she talked about the pastor's quirkiness to all of the ladies she knew. She warned them not to do anything for the pastor unless they wanted to see him angry because they "didn't do it just right." That wasn't a super fair assessment of the pastor or his motives, but it sure felt that way to Tina.

Six months later and still feeling a bit bruised and shy about volunteering in any capacity, Tina walked into the church and saw posters hanging advertising a women's ministry event. The posters were hand drawn with stick figures. Tina was furious that they had been allowed to be displayed. She went to the pastor to ask how these posters were any different from hers.

In fact, they were quite different. The posters may have been hand drawn, but they were drawn by a cartoon artist named Georgia who had done work on the side for Marvel. They were not thrown together haphazardly but rather had had about twenty hours put into them. They were not taped to the wall with scotch tape; they were mounted and framed and placed on easels.

It wasn't about the pen and paper. Quite frankly, this story has nothing to do with art or creativity. Regardless of who is right or wrong in this story (and there is fault in both directions), the fact remains that all people involved would have been well served by a clearly defined plumbline in regard to excellence.

If we believe it is part of our role to teach people a theology of beauty and aesthetic, we need to articulate some guidelines. We may have varying opinions about what is pretty or artistic, but honoring a standard of excellence is a wonderful way to begin that conversation. It is easier to recognize something that looks like it took little or no effort than it is to judge something as beautiful or not.

With all this said, there is part of me that detests the word excellence. There have been instances in the past when members of our own staff have held this plumbline against us as leaders: "They only care about perfection." However, we haven't found a better word to describe the motivation and intentionality we believe should be present in everything we do. We don't want people to assume we look at things only in light of our idea of what perfection is.

What concerns us more than falling short of anyone's specific idea of perfection is apathy. The rub is not when the end product is not perfect. The rub is when the end product obviously falls way short of that person's abilities or what was mutually agreed upon, or when there is an attitude of indifference, lack of effort, or outright insubordination.

Sometimes accusing someone of expecting too much or being a control freak is an easy way out of apathy. Just like telling someone you'll pray for him or her is an easy way out of a conversation. We don't want to elevate the concept of excellence (as defined by our idea of what is perfect) to the point that it becomes a preoccupation and cause for stress. But there needs to be some kind of standard.

True confessions: this is easier said than done. I *am* at times a control freak. I have very specific ideas. I am very opinionated.

At times, I have struggled way too hard to raise the bar from A to A+, not realizing the cost to my own health and the health of those around me.

If you have a problem letting go of anything short of your own idea of perfection (like I have at times), it is a sin issue (as it is in me). This doesn't mean, however, that a leader should throw out the standard-of-excellence-baby with the control-freak bathwater. Pray. Seek help. Learn to breathe. Don't hold so tightly to the reins. And, at the same time, don't settle for apathy.

We practice every Thursday evening with our church band. The band practices on its own time as well. Some band members are in lessons throughout the week even though they already know how to play. We have a little slogan we sometimes like to repeat when practice becomes difficult: God is worth our best. The team is worth our best. The people are worth our best.

Plumbline #17 Imagination Is Godly

Creativity is paramount in everything. It's one of the ways we shadow God. Therefore, we will often try new things "just because" and, unlike many others, we change for the sake of change—just to keep things fresh and fluid. We seldom do the same thing twice, and we take art seriously—it's much more than either advertising or propaganda; it's creativity made flesh in honor of the Creator.

When we talk out loud about this plumbline in church circles, someone inevitably asks, "What if you don't have creative people at your church?" Or, "What if our church doesn't have the kind of budget your church has for creative things?"

First, we believe everyone has the capacity to be creative to some degree. As image bearers of God, we believe we carry part of the Creator inside of us. Man's first act after he was created by God was to name the animals—a creative act. Art, song, business deals, playtime, conversation, dreams, imagination, and work ethic, to name a few, can all be creative acts that mirror God. Simply being faithful to share your personal story of redemption is a creative act as you bear the Imago Dei.

The real question behind the question of creativity is, "What if my church doesn't have artists?" This is an entirely different question. I have always been part of a church body that is ripe with artists. In all honesty, it's not because I'm lucky. It takes hard work to foster an environment of art.

Remember, these are our plumblines I'm sharing with you to spark conversation and get you thinking about what you believe. We do value art and are blessed with quite a few artists presently. Art needs to be addressed in different ways for us than it does for some churches. Please don't hear me saying that if your church is not artistic, you are something less than you could be.

But many of the churches I know of with an artist deficit are not really doing a lot to welcome artists. They believe God will drop artists into their laps. While he may do that for some, let me suggest the following things for you to consider:

Pray for artists.

Seek out artists.

Spend time in the art centers of your city.

Invite artists to participate in what you do.

Hold art contests to design your logos/posters/space.

Become part of art clubs and organizations in your city.

Place ads in your paper and online, searching for artists.

Host concerts at your church.

Buy local art.

Have your meetings in coffee shops. Artists live there.

Send kids in your church to art school.

Look for interns in the colleges of your area.

Contact the high school art department.

Don't think of art simply in terms of advertisement or propaganda.

Hire an artist on staff. Even part-time. Or spare-time.

Ask local churches to borrow their art.

Open your church as a gallery.

Raise money for a local art school.

Wear a t-shirt around town that says, "Are you an artist?"

Outsource.

Read books that broaden your understanding of art and artists.

Quit calling it "decoration." The artists might start believing you care.

Develop an art budget. Put your money where your mouth is.

As to the question of financial resources, you'd be surprised how little you can spend to make something beautiful. A can of paint doesn't cost a whole lot. Yet many of the churches I hear complain about lack of artists or not having enough money to be creative are screaming out from the insides of white coffins. Get a dang roller dirty with paint.

We all dream of having unlimited resources, but honestly, we've had Industrial Light and Magic dreams on a RadioShack budget for as long as I can remember.

Ask people to fund art projects.

Ask folks for free crap around their homes.

Go to yard sales.

Watch HGTV and DIY and . . .

Recycle materials.

Subscribe to magazines with cheap ideas.

Walk around Lowes and ask, "What can we make with this?"

Borrow.

Don't make excuses.

Plumbline #18 We Grow Our Own "We"

We are suspect of things made "over there" and then brought willy-nilly "over here" (e.g., conference materials), because where they came from ought to tie directly into the unique situational requirements for why they were made in the first place. Because ministry comes from within you, we want our people to make their own stuff. "Indie" is cool. We don't copy-cat, and we don't like pre-packaged items/materials. If God is really alive and at work in you, then what you do ought to flow out into your own expression and brand of ministry.

Bryce started in professional ministry right after he graduated from a Bible university and seminary in Portland, Oregon. He was fired up to start a church and grow a community. Bryce is a musician, and back when he started in ministry, he had a group of about fifteen or twenty musicians eager to start the church with him. They had no money. They had a dream and a calling and a burning desire to foster a community of people in the Pacific Northwest.

They met in an old pub when they started. Ministry looked like bonfires at Bryce's house, playing music in local bars and having times of spiritual conversation afterward, vegetarian potlucks, and lawn games on Sunday afternoon.

The pub allowed them to hang original art on the walls, which scratched an itch for both parties. Kids' ministry was thoughtful, creative, and well planned, but it wasn't really flashy. In Bryce's mind, it didn't need to be. It needed to be fun, engaging, interesting, and something the kids would talk about when they went home to their parents.

Bryce would take long walks around his neighborhood at night and talk to people walking their dogs and sitting on their porches as he passed by. He would sometimes ask them if they had a church they belonged to. If they said no, he would give them an invitation to join the community he and his friends had started. No pressure. Bryce called this "farming" his neighborhood.

Over the years, the church outgrew the pub and ended up in an old church building. Then an old school. They grew to a couple hundred people, but they were watching those numbers slowly decline. They certainly weren't growing at all.

The music at the church was good quality, but it sounded much different from when they had started fifteen years prior in that old pub. Their indie-rock sound and indigenous worship full of songs written by local musicians was replaced with worship song standards their music leader got from his networks and conferences.

Their kids' ministry was struggling to survive. The curriculum they purchased from a distributor was decent enough, but the teachers weren't real excited about teaching it, and it showed.

The drama ministry was failing fast. Though they didn't have drama when they started the church, it had been suggested they start a program about ten years into their journey. Now, the struggle to come up with a good drama every week was killing their small team of volunteers.

119

One day, Bryce went out to lunch with his friend who was also a pastor. Bryce told him, "This is not what I signed up for." He explained that the ministry did not look anything like his original vision, and it was hard to cheerlead something that didn't feel true to his personality.

His friend told him, "Tough. This is not about what you signed up for. This is about you being faithful to the call of Jesus. The kingdom is not all about your personal tastes. Quit whining and get back to work."

His friend was only partly right. Ministry is hard, and if we ever feel like we can totally relax and there is no controversy, we are probably in need of a change. Yes, no whining. Yes, it's not "all about personal taste."

But has there ever been a ministry design that totally ignores personal taste? Is it all about function? Is there a system that exists that everyone will gravitate toward regardless of preference? The answer Bryce's friend gave him assumed his current ministry style was one that should work for everyone and Bryce should submit to it. And he gave Bryce the dangerous directive to be okay with being stagnant.

Quirky leadership would have a different answer for Bryce. Bryce sold out. He sold out to an idea of ministry he thought he was supposed to be doing because everyone else was doing it. He forgot along the way that there is no prescription for ministry style in scripture. Scripture gives an incredible amount of freedom in designing ministries.

Somewhere along the way, Bryce lost his unique ministry perspective and sidelined the unique people who were walking alongside him. His church was on the rapid decline, due in no small part to the fact that his ethos was lacking. No one believed what he was selling. Not even him.

Of course he loves Jesus. Of course he loves people. But he was no longer speaking the language he was fluent in.

Bryce's ministry lacked integrity. He had allowed the ministry he was called to lead to become something he was entirely unfamiliar with and even opposed to in many ways. He had allowed a ministry to be created for someone "out there" based on what he heard was working in other churches. Somewhere.

In an effort to be hands-off and permission giving, Bryce had allowed people to run with the ideas they had learned about at church conferences and books they read on ministry. While permission giving is valiant (as opposed to being a total control freak), Bryce had sacrificed all the things he believed to be true about ministry in his context to the beast of popular church culture.

In the evangelical American church today, we can safely assume a few standard things will be present in most every Christian church ministry that meets regularly in a building (as opposed to house churches). Of course, size, denomination, financial means, location, and building limitations will flavor these elements, but for the most part we will find:

A weekly message

Corporate music

Announcements

Offering

Ushers

Children's ministry

Quirky leadership says even the above elements, which seem elementary and maybe even necessary for some, are up for grabs. I'm not saying they need to be done away with by any means. However, while I'm sure someone might have a well-developed theology of worship that states the importance of corporate singing and the preaching of the word, we'd be hard-pressed to make a case for those things being mandated as something that happens weekly or within a specific timeframe.

When Bryce started in ministry, he never asked himself, "How am I going to make sure I have all these elements covered?" His questions were much different. They are the questions Bryce should be asking now in his time of holy discontent:

Who am I?

How has God shaped me to lead?

What people live in my town?

Who are my friends?

What are my friends listening to, reading, and watching?

What are the needs in my town?

Who are the unlovely, and how do I love them?

What is *not* important to us as a community?

How does the place in which I live shape people's lifestyles?

Who are the committed people I do life with, and how are they shaped?

What are my people currently doing to minister in the community?

How do people in my community learn and process information?

What do I believe is tired and old?

What is my story?

What has not worked in the past?

INDIGENOUS MINISTRY

Some synonyms for *indigenous* are *native, original, local,* and *home-grown.* This is why we say we "grow our own 'WE.'"

I'd like to take a look at indigenous home-grown ministry through the lens of music. It's an easy one for me to use as a musician, and I think it will be easy for you to gravitate toward as well, even if you aren't.

Some time ago, every church I know was singing Matt Redman's "Heart of Worship." I love the story behind the song. Matt told us when we were in Ireland a few years back that it came out of an experience in his own church. They recognized that while they were contributing to a worship music revival of sorts, they had somehow found themselves wandering and trying to find meaning in their own musical expression.

And so the words . . .

"I'm coming back to the heart of worship, and it's all about You . . . I'm sorry Lord for the thing I've made it . . ."

Beautiful song. I'm sure many identified with it. In many ways, I did personally. It was a song born out of a particular experience. From a particular franchise of the kingdom. It hit a nerve with many churches, and they embraced it.

But we never sang it at Westwinds.

Because it wasn't us.

When the song came out, Westwinds was not concerned about coming back to the heart of worship. There was no coming "back." Many hadn't been there.

There is great pressure in the church music world to sing the next new thing put out by the latest and greatest of worship music artists. The latest song pimped at a conference. The next song by "that person."

And some of the songs are amazing. I think most are not.

Every once in a while, I find a gem that surprises me like a stray dog on the porch. I take it in and keep it forever. But, honestly, most of it sounds the same to me or doesn't speak to our individual experience.

I know this sounds cynical to some of you. Fair enough. I am at times. But this is not a rant about the motives of the industry or artists. My concern is for the church. Do we really believe what we are singing? Do the songs we sing resonate with our people?

Too often, songs are introduced to our churches simply because they are available and easy and they're getting airplay on the Christian station. But that doesn't make them good. And even if a song is good, it doesn't mean we should be singing it.

Over the years, we have celebrated MANY songs written by some great artists. We have sung them shoulder to shoulder with many churches across the world. Many have become anthems for the kingdom. But I would argue that much of what we sing in our churches is what we think we "should" be singing. Because all the cool kids are. Or because "that" artist wrote it and he/she is "anointed." Or because a label or organization is pimping it.

In many cases, I feel like the church is eating the cafeteria hot lunch it is being served because it signed up for the cheap meal plan. The food is accessible and affordable, so we just consume it.

We need to get in the kitchen.

It's troubling how homogenized, uniform, similar, streamlined, and packaged our corporate worship has become in the church world. It's an assembly line. It's Costco. It's IKEA. It's clip art.

The church *system* has molded artists into its own image. Conferences and books that resource, spark ideas, create camaraderie, and inspire are all good things. But in some cases, the fallout of being so connected to the world around us is that we are losing our ability to create on our own. We don't have to dream.

We don't have to read the signs. It's easy to let someone else discern what is good, what is mediocre, and what is crap.

We are losing our ability to foster creative environments, respond to what is going on around us, speak into the chaos, and create commentary and discussion in light of our local church experience.

Is it wrong to cover the latest Chris Tomlin song in church? Absolutely not. It might be perfect. But if we sit back and consume what an industry is giving us without question and kid ourselves into thinking, "It must be good because everyone else is singing it," we are slowly dying.

If we constantly allow someone else to tell us what our congregation needs, we are missing out. And we are probably lazy. We are killing our imaginations.

We spend more time thinking about how to copy the chord progressions and find the right inversions of chords than we do dreaming, searching, and making.

I have always had a love/hate relationship with popular church music. Part of me feels a great amity with other churches when I know I can travel across the world and sing the same songs churches in my area sing. Part of me feels immediately comfortable, as if I am part of something bigger than the local franchise I belong to. It's fun to go to conferences where everyone knows the same songs.

The part of me that rejects popular church music sits at a conference where they turn Crowder into chowder. Or when I am at a Latino church with a full percussion/hand drum/bongo/conga section that covers Chris Tomlin and forces his 6/8 song in the key of A flat into a 4/4 salsa structure. This is all part of ethos. It's obvious when it doesn't ring true.

Not too long ago, I got asked by a middle-class, white missionary to go to Africa and teach some worship pastors songs "in the vein of Worship Together/Vineyard/Maranatha! Music." It would have been a great opportunity, but I was heartbroken over how they wanted me to go about helping them.

The indigenous music of the African culture is beautiful but absolutely nothing like what they wanted me to teach. I told them I would consider coming over and teaching them to be the best possible "them" they could be. I would teach them to listen to the music of their culture and emulate and celebrate it.

They refused. They said they wanted to "resource" the pastors, not teach them my philosophy of worship.

I can think of few worse musical blunders than teaching an African band how to play (or even rearrange) popular white-bread-soccer-mom worship tunes. This is what Promise Keepers did a few years back with a Latino version of "Lord, I Lift Your Name on High." Painful.

We are more concerned about getting product into people's hands so they can in turn share the product. We buy the product that is marketed to us because it is easy and accessible. We often choose our music like some choose "art" for their homes by going to Kmart and buying a Thomas Kinkade print. Pre-framed. From the bin. But the problem here isn't about taste. There is a deeper systemic problem within the church world: complacency.

Ministry folk don't need to be artists, or thinkers, or poets, or prophets, or orators, or leaders anymore. In the system of ministry we've allowed to happen to us, we don't have to be proactive. We don't necessarily even have to work on honing our skills. We just have to know where to go to buy simple, accessible, easily reproducible music. Or download sermons. Or capture video from the internet.

I saw an ad recently in which a church was looking for a worship leader. The description of the person went something like this: "Mid to late twenties, familiar with popular worship music, preferably leads from guitar."

That was it. *oR Christ!*

Nothing about craft, art, self-motivation, creativity, taste, experience, philosophy, or skill. Nothing about familiarity with the music culture of the church seeking to fill the position. Nothing about the music culture of the town the church was in. Just someone who could reproduce the recipe.

I wonder how it would fly if we searched for senior pastors the same way? "Thirty-five to forty-five years old, able to reproduce popular sermons, preferably speaks from a manuscript."

In many cases, the worship band has become a jukebox.

Imagine what could happen in churches if musicians approached the music like a good preacher approaches a sermon: taking the temperature of the church, asking God what he wants to say to the people, collecting stories and writing them down, retelling stories, studying, researching, not settling for the same thing they said last week, speaking the language of the culture.

Certainly, there are wonderful pieces of music that should be considered for your own church's corporate worship. You don't have to write it all yourself. There are a lot of songs to choose from. They don't have to be Top Ten songs. They don't have to be getting airplay on Christian radio. They don't have to be written by a *worship* artist.

We need some metrics for discerning what music choices are best for our local franchise of the church. As you read through this list, ask how these questions are applicable to *all* the ministries in your church.

---

1. Does this reflect my church's personality?

2. Do people in my town actually enjoy this kind of music, or do they step into church and hear a totally different thing than they are used to hearing? Where do I live? Is this music foreign to my people? (It's okay to celebrate new genres of music for sure, but don't force a genre into a culture as a norm).

3. What is the most popular radio station in my area? Might I think about more songs that reflect that style?

4. Are there musicians in my church who are good at doing another style of music, and can I invite them to share their gift with us? (Where are the rappers?)

5. Do the lyrics really reflect something our church understands and embraces? If not, am I willing to teach through it? Do I teach through songs for the benefit of non-believers? Is the song's language a barrier to the non-believer?

6. Just because 175 worship music CDs have this song on it, does it mean it's good?

7. Do the lyrics make sense? Are they intelligent or dumb? Are they forcing rhymes or saying something that matters? (I don't think all songs have to teach something.)

8. Is the song actually biblical? Have I checked that out?

9. Is this song saying anything new or different? Or is it the same thing we've been saying over and over in the same way?

10. Does this song sound the same as everything else we do (key of G, 4/4, four on the floor, aptly placed solo, etc.)?

11. Does it stretch our creativity and require us to play anything other than strumming and hitting something?

12. Am I doing this song simply because everyone else is, or do I really like the song?

13. Does this song have the same kind of rhyming conventions as everything else, or is it doing something different from rhyming "face" with "place"?

14. Does this song sound just like the other songs this guy did? If so, why would I want to do this one?

15. Is this song true to who I AM as a musician? Or do I think I have to be something I am not in order to be a worship musician?

16. When I do this song, do the people actually respond to it in any way, tell me they like it, sing along, or give me any clue we should keep doing it? Should I drop it?

GET REAL

And so it is with ministry. Period. Music. Preaching. Corporate worship. Outreach. Programs. The choices we make about the initiatives we fund. The way we structure our budget. The positions we staff. *Resting within a system we have in part created and allowed to happen to us is weakening our ethos.*

Telling someone else's story and using someone else's methods is numbing our integrity. And when you're offering hope to the hopeless, your integrity is all you've got.

There may be ministries in your church that are flailing and barely existing because no one believes in them. Worst of all, you don't.

Maybe you think they're weak ministries. Shallow. A waste of time and money. Embarrassing. Off-mission. You don't think they fit in your community, speak to real needs, or are an accurate reflection of your church personality, and you certainly wouldn't dream them up and fund them if you had any say.

But you DO have a say.

And, most likely, YOUR say is the say of others as well who haven't been given the freedom to pull the plug. Most likely, your say is what needs to happen to liberate people who feel stuck in a place they don't want to be but feel compelled by guilt or stagnated by tradition. Your say can free up resources and create new energy to do the things you know you should be doing or at least want to try.

Most likely, your say is going to make some people angry as well. But what is more painful: short-term conflict resolution and fallout or a lifetime of oppression in which tails wag dogs?

One of my favorite game shows I watched as a kid was "To Tell the Truth." Three challengers are introduced at the top of the show, all claiming to be the same person. The host asks them, "What is your name, please?" Each challenger then states, "My name is [central character's name]." Celebrity panelists ask a series of questions trying to determine who the real central character is. Challengers can lie, but the real character is sworn "to tell the truth."

The celebrities vote on who they think the real person is, and the host announces, "Will the real [person's name] please stand up?"

The real central character then stands after some playful partial ups and downs of the three contestants designed to build tension as we await the big reveal. The two fake characters or "imposters" then expose their real names and their true occupations. Prize money is awarded to the challengers based on the number of incorrect votes the *impostors* draw.

Quirky leaders can't waste time and energy as imposters. There is no prize big enough. We can't pretend to be what we're not, and we can't be caught leading what is not a part of us. People will sniff it out (and they should). We can pretend for only so long. Even our short-term successes will leave us wanting and may set the stage for long-term disappointment as our ministries take on a life of their own and serve themselves.

What are the rewards for being real as a leader and as a church? We sleep better at night knowing we are on task and our people are finding fulfillment, and we get to have life-changing conversations with people who believe in what we are saying and doing because we actually believe in those things too.

We find new energy to do the stuff God has incubated in us, sometimes over the course of many years, because our headspace is not cluttered with the things we manage just because someone else told us we should be sustaining them.

We suddenly find time to cheerlead things that matter and are making a difference. Gone are the questions from people about why you don't give "their" ministry any face time.

We make new friends because people like to watch fires burn and they want to follow leaders who are animated by what is thriving and by what opportunities lie ahead.

The church budget becomes a living part of the organism. Guilt about where money is being spent is a thing of the past.

We see people come out of hiding and make themselves available to help because there is cause.

Our mission rhymes with the saints of the past who have understood the most effective ministries are kingdom franchise specific. For your people. For the place where we live. As we were made to be.

CHAPTER SIX:
I'll HAVE WHAT SHE'S HAVING

Your church is going to fail. That's what everyone tells you. Most of the time you believe it's your fault. You believe it's your own sin, rebellion, misalignment, and failure to be a certain brand of leader in a certain brand of church, and many times you allow yourself to believe *that leader* and *that church* exist outside of your particular gifts and abilities. There's hope. You're wrong.

There's a famous scene in the classic *When Harry Met Sally* where a woman observes Meg Ryan pretending she is having an orgasm (don't pretend you don't know the scene I'm talking about) in the restaurant they are seated in. When Ryan's character finishes her public display, the woman exclaims, "I'll have what she's having." In some ways, some church leaders have a lot in common with the restaurant woman.

Desperate for anything that might work, grasping for a handhold, longing for the next great thing that might rescue us, we're willing to try anything if it looks like it's working for someone else. We certainly can learn from each other and should, but it's bothersome that some of us fight for "what she's having" and defend it as the right choice as long as what she's having is popular and makes the most sense at the time. We'll surrender our own opinions and gut instincts for the popular menu choice when someone or enough people make a scene or shriek about it.

But the menu's changing all the time. We waste a lot of time fighting about the right way to do church and ignore the ways in which we can make our church more effective in our particular flavor. God's promise to Abraham was that nations would be blessed through him. God's promise to you is that people will be blessed through your church in only the way your church can bless.

What do you already believe about church? What are your gut beliefs? You're at the table and everyone is asking, "What are you having?"

Plumbline #19 The Church Is God's Plan A; There Is No Plan B

This is where people are changed and resourced and transformed. As much as there is distinction between ecclesiology (every Christian person is part of God's church) and actuality (the local churches are not wholly filled with every Christian person), it's important to recognize that—for better or for worse—the local church is all we've got to heal the world. Every Christian person needs to be in a church in actuality, not just jump through an ecclesiological loophole and opt out. For our part, as leaders within the church, we want to drive all our efforts at getting more people here, because we can't do anything to help them become better followers of Jesus until they start showing up more frequently. After all, you can't clean a fish that's not in the boat.

Both "The Church is God's plan A; There is no plan B" and "You can't clean a fish that's not in the boat" are phrases we stole from somewhere. We don't really know where from. But I say that just so *we* come clean.

A while back, we had a group at the church we lovingly refer to as "The Dissenters." They were a hilarious group of Bible college kids who were very vocal about the fact that we were doing church "all wrong." They had a whole mess of Bible verses they found and strung together while doing their hermeneutical aerobics that "proved" our model of church was extra-biblical at best. They were wrong about the dots they connected in scripture, but that's a different story.

What was disconcerting (although a bit charming too) was the way they expressed their discontent. They all gathered in a corner of the lobby during The Cue (that's what we call our Sunday gathering) and talked and prayed. Though they were never really disruptive in an obnoxious and loud (volume) kind of a way, they were clearly sending a *loud* (attitude) message to the leadership by not participating in anything.

A defining moment in *The Saga of Westwinds and the Dissenters* was a brilliant move orchestrated by David McDonald and our youth pastor, Ben Redmond. One Sunday (when I was speaking and not David), the two of them decided the best way to meet the passive aggression of the group was to surprise them with a luncheon. David and Ben delivered trays of food and drink to the space in the lobby where they met and invited them to talk things through.

The looks on their faces were evidence that they expected the fight to go much differently than to be met with hospitality. Surprised, and a bit embarrassed, they fumbled through their misgivings and disillusions.

They told David and Ben they were like a house church. They were doing church a different way. "Like Jesus intended and like the first church." But their house church didn't meet in a house at all. They met in the building we provided. And that meeting place was clearly chosen to send us a message.

And, because they were not involved in any ministry at the church nor were they volunteering in any capacity in the community we live in, their beef was clearly and specifically with the way we do The Cue—not really about how church should be done, how it should grow, how people are discipled, etc. In the course of the luncheon, this truth came out. They admitted they didn't like large groups and they wanted a more verse-by-verse teaching method, more ancient hymns, and public prayer requests (to name a few).

The group of people eventually left our church. They said they no longer felt welcome. In fact, they were very welcome here, but we did make it known they weren't welcome to picket silently in our lobby anymore.

On their way out, some of them said, "We don't really need the church anyway to be Christians." Really? When we start basing our decisions on what we don't have to do, what we can get by with, and what is absolutely necessary to get a passing grade, we start down a long road of discontent and entitlement.

Furthermore, who said we don't need the church? It wasn't Jesus. It wasn't Paul. It wasn't anyone in the entire New Testament. Who is this guru who allows our personal preference to supersede the standard of scripture?

You don't have to go to MY church to be a Christian. That's for sure. But to say you don't need THE church is to make yourself an orphan twice removed.

"Live together. Die alone."
—Jack, from ABC's *Lost*

We have no problem with house churches. Or cell churches. Or churches that meet once a month in a corporate gathering. Or hymns. Or group prayer requests. I'm guessing you don't have problems with these either. But God has called us to lead a specific group of people in a specific fashion. The way we are particularly shaped. That group of people meets weekly at the corner of Robinson and McCain roads in Jackson, Michigan. It is God and that group we stand accountable to. We are not a house church, and we should not be ashamed if we don't tickle a particular fancy that someone's idea of the perfect house church does.

The church at large has far too many young, angry, independent, opinionated, and immature folks flipping off the church. Forgetting she is the bride. With all her flaws. With all her scars. We all contribute to her unlovely parts that God chooses to call beautiful.

Plumbline #20 The Church Is Not a Provider of Religious Goods and Services

The church isn't "for you." You are meant to shadow God. You are meant to heal the world. The church is not here to "meet your needs," and it's not our job to feed you. You need to learn to "pick up a spoon" and feed yourself.

Scott adopted a teenage boy. The boy was rejected by his birth family. He's "too much to handle" for them. Scott graciously took him in though he can barely provide for himself.

Scott is an extremely hard worker. Blue-collar laborer. Self-employed. Always wondering where the next paycheck is coming from by nature of his profession. As such, he found his cupboard nearly bare a few times this winter. One weekend, some couples pulled together and bought him enough food to last a couple of months. They filled his pantry with a variety of food. He was speechless. He and his son had just gone without food for a couple of days without telling anyone.

The day after the pantry filling, he got a call at work from his adopted son. "There is nothing to eat in this house," he said. Scott asked, "What do you mean there is nothing to eat? There is a cupboard full of food. Make yourself something." His son replied, "I don't want to make anything. I just want to eat."

Far too many Christians want food made for them. They don't want to look around at the ingredients and get their hands dirty. They want someone to package their meal for them.

"Well, then," Scott said, "Eat some cereal."

"I don't want to eat that food," his son replied. "I want some chicken."

Far too many Christians are screaming, "You don't feed me the way I want to be fed."

And far too many pastors carry guilt for not meeting every whiny and spoiled child's demands.

As quirky leaders, we must not fall into the trap of being short-order cooks. When my wife cooks dinner (and she is, by the way, one fine chef), it is what the kids eat. No one gets to shout out his or her order. We shouldn't apologize when we don't offer a particular side.

We are not a smorgasbord. Smorgies never excel at any one thing. They do a bunch of things blandly. Cheap and easy. To try to please everyone. We can't let our churches become the all-you-can-eat botulism bin where everyone gorges until they puke. It's not sustainable. It's not healthy. And no chef ever feels fulfilled there, either.

Plumbline #21 Church Should Be More Church-Like, Not Business-Like

Corporate culture subtly undercuts the mission of the church. The church should not be cultured like IBM, even though there are business aspects to the management of the church's resources.

Over the years, we have had to interpret and take liberty with our own policies in light of specific circumstances. When policies affect people, those people's circumstances sometimes dictate a closer look at the policy. Such has been the case with staff members who have had cancer, knee surgeries, sin issues, loss of loved ones, home foreclosures, clinical depression, marital complications, and various nearly incapacitating seasons of life.

Where corporate culture sometimes says, "Such is life," and reconciles decisions based on bottom lines, precedence, and public pressure, we dare to be different. Quirky leadership is one that holds rules loosely and sometimes bends them dramatically because people are worth it, and the end result is something much more beautiful than toeing the line.

The quirky leader doesn't care how things are interpreted in the corporate world as much as he or she cares about how people are falling more in love with Jesus. He or she doesn't bow to the pressures of businesspeople who say, "The church is a business too!" The quirky leader understands that conventional stewardship rules often add up to 1 + 1 = 0. This is not some footloose and fancy-free ticket to carelessness by any means, but sometimes wisdom wins over convention. Even if that convention was founded on the wisdom of another time. Mercy triumphs over judgment.

I have a friend in San Francisco who is an associate pastor. He confessed to a pornography addiction to his senior pastor one day despite fear of losing his job and his credibility. On many church staffs, he would have been thrown out the door before he could say, "Let he who is without sin . . ." Instead, his senior pastor bent the conventional rules, denied the pressure of potential public opinion, and went out on a limb. He invited my friend and his wife to take some time off to heal and communicate without the pressures of work. The church paid for them to go through counseling to heal some brokenness and communicate. My friend walked a long road of healing with his church while staying on staff. His senior pastor is a quirky leader who dared to ask, "Who said I have to fire this guy?"

Plumbline #22 We Are a Voice of Prophetic Reorientation

We need to critique reality, to confront those things within the church that are not the way God wants them to be. Church is not about keeping people happy. We need to be truth tellers, reminding people that things should be different. Our role within the kingdom is to speak about change for the future. Convention doesn't pressure us. We understand that if we are faithful in discharging our mission, it will likely anger religious people.

When someone says the word "prophet," we immediately think of the prophets of the First Testament. The prophets were God's mouthpiece (sometimes bullhorn) to the people. They interpreted the past and present and spoke the future as God revealed and they interpreted. The tenor of the prophet depended on personality and the occasion, so in scripture we imagine prophets looking and sounding like everything from Wolf Blitzer to Steve Jobs to Gandalf to David Blaine.

God too has given us as leaders specific personalities, places, and occasions to speak into. The role is the same, though we all look different and live in different places.

Like the prophets of old, we believe we have a role of seeing and communicating what is not readily seen by others, if it is seen at all. We look at things as they are in light of what we know they should be and point our Holy Spirit-shaped finger at it and say, "This does not ring true."

But it is not always a negative role in that it stands *against* what is readily seen. More so, the prophetic voice stands *for* what can and should be. Part of the role is interpretive. Putting flesh on something. Or, as we like to say sometimes (because it conjures up visions of all the sci-fi things we love), the prophetic role is one that *animates* what's not there.

Prophetic reorientation is often about upsetting the apple cart. Firing up the imagination. Waking up the sedentary world that is dressed in its proper three-piece religious suit and dressing it once again with its underwear on the outside of its pants as it imagines a world where superheroes are alive and well, dragons are slain, damsels are rescued from distress, and magic exists.

Prophetic reorientation says things in ways they've never been said and deconstructs what is widely accepted as standard operating procedure. It is okay with tension and lives in a world that creates space for the discovery of truth through art, metaphor, and image. Prophetic reorientation does not settle for "This is the way it's always been said," especially if those words have lost their meaning and effect.

The prophet leader is very intentional about using language that makes sense to people. He or she realizes that language changes all around us constantly and we, as the church, need to be ahead of the curve. A perfect example of this is some of the church's reticence to accept social networking platforms as real community—dismissing them altogether instead of thinking that perhaps there is just a new kind of community evolving. It doesn't have to replace the old one. But it can't be ignored, or one day we will no longer be able to communicate anymore.

The prophets of the First Testament were not always popular. Oh, I'm sure someone thought it was cool that Hosea married a prostitute or that Ezekiel used poop as prophetic performance art, but honestly, prophets piss off religious people.

One of my favorite prophetic moments on a weekend at Westwinds happened when David was speaking about going through *tough times*. David took a trip to a farm on Saturday and collected buckets of manure. As he was giving the message, he lifted the lids from the buckets, and the smell of fresh excrement wafted over the people like a trip down I-5 through the San Joaquin Valley in the California heat (trust me, if you haven't taken that route, rolling up the windows doesn't help).

141

As if that wasn't uncomfortable enough, David was picking it up with his bare hands and squishing it through his fingers, sometimes flinging it as he talked. He had no control over where the poo got flung, but there was no doubt who was flinging the poo. David captured our attention in that moment as he described for us how it's the, ahem, manure of life that makes us grow.

While many thought it was brilliant (me included), many did not like the surprise. Especially the ladies in the dresses who sat in the Shamu splash-zone up front. But prophetic reorientation isn't always comfortable or predictable.

Because the prophet is ready to interpret and receive instruction from God that is unconventional at times, he or she is often without the approval of peers. Some churches want to take the prophets home, clean them up, shave their wild hairs, reprogram them, and teach them to process and speak clearly and slowly.

There are groups of Christians who scoff at us because of what we do at Westwinds. And what we don't do. Admittedly, what we do and do not do at times is intentional to the degree that we are trying to raise awareness. We are trying to rattle cages. We are trying to point out the emperor is not wearing clothes. We are trying to point out the big pink elephant in the room (enter any other metaphor here you would like). Sometimes our role as quirky leaders is to take action on the things we know will go against the grain (more overused metaphors) and make us the only salmon swimming downstream (okay, I'm done).

We cannot halt from moving in a direction in which God is calling us simply because of the pain that might come our way from onlookers outside of our context and people who think they know better. When you are led to do something that may seem controversial to some, your first obligation is to help the people in your church navigate the minefield—the ones you are responsible to. You may or may not have an obligation to explain yourself to other churches, depending on whether you are doing something unbiblical, illegal, or against the guidelines of the denomination to which you have submitted.

Pick your battles. Choose wisely. Then fight hard. This is the role of the prophet. Because people coming to Jesus actually matters, your prophetic voice matters.

The prophetic voice is important in grand-scale endeavors and mundane conversation. Prophets speak truth truthfully in every situation and to every occasion. Your congregation needs your prophetic voice. Yes, we need each other's to some degree as well, but YOUR congregation needs your voice. More than ever. Voices are coming at them from every angle. Speak truth. Speak it truthfully.

In our experience, prophetic conversation and instruction will be PG-13 or R sometimes, because that's the world we are speaking into. Jesus didn't come to seek and save the behavior and mindset of a G-rated world.

Unless you are particularly offensive for the sake of being offensive, don't change your tone of prophetic voice. Your church needs your quirky style. When I taught communication labs for a college, this was one of the hardest things to get through to aspiring orators—use your real voice. Not your radio voice. Not your CNN voice. Your real voice goes beyond tone and inflection; it's the "how you would normally say things" part of you.

David McDonald, my partner in crime, said it like this once in a post he made on his blog shadowinggod.com:

> I've always considered my refusal to speak differ-
> ently in different situations as a kind of merit badge.
> Truthfully, that has cost me in my career—it seems
> that many people want a young, hip provocateur for
> a pastor who is also suave, genteel, and eloquent
> when dolled up in a suit and asked to say a prayer at
> some public dinner.

But I have no desire to be so duplicitous. And—thankfully—I think much of our world has grown tired of seeing people act one way at home and another at church, or school, or work, or whatever.

So, whether it's the weekend message or a conversation over a beer with us, you are going to get . . . us. Your people should get . . . you.

Plumbline #23 Corporate Worship Events Are Meant to be Aggregates and Gateways for All People to Experience God

Church is not just for believers, but neither is it all about seekers. Our church attracts the spiritually curious, the disenfranchised (those burned out on organized religion), thinkers, and creatives. It's for everybody to better encounter their Creator, and thus it utilizes multi-sensory worship and incorporates differing learning styles (visual, aural, kinesthetic). Furthermore, we play with extra-biblical models knowing that there is no "right" way to pray and there is no biblical prescription for weekend worship.

While most of us would probably agree that what happens on the weekend in our church services is not the most important thing we do as a church, many of us sell the weekend service short. Sure, the church is not all about the weekend service. But it counts. One of the easiest ways to determine what a church believes about ministry is to sit through 65 minutes of sermon and song with them on a Sunday.

Music choices, aesthetics and décor, length of sermon, room arrangement, lighting, the presence or lack of art, the design of bulletins and screen announcements, the elements of the service, the length of the service all tell a story about your church's ministry philosophy. So it's easy to start here when examining and articulating ministry plumblines.

We should be very clear about what we believe about what happens on the weekend. It's easy to come to the conclusion that, in most cases, the only people who ever care about or challenge your beliefs about weekend philosophy are Christians from other churches who believe things should be different, because they are the most vocal. In many cases, however, there are people in your church who are *very* committed to the ministry as a whole but have questions about the choices you make on the weekend.

In an effort to get you to think through your own philosophy of ministry in the big picture, I want to give you an idea of what we believe about the weekend services at Westwinds. Feel free to poke holes, take notes, adapt, and question. As you do all these things, ask yourself, "Why do I believe this?"

Often, we are asked about our philosophy of ministry when it comes to The Cue—our weekend gathering at Westwinds. For those who are new to church, the atmosphere may not be what they expected, but they are usually pleasantly surprised. For those who grew up in a traditional evangelical or mainline denomination, the atmosphere is familiar in some ways and Titanically different from what some expect or are used to.

At The Cue, our aim is to facilitate an environment—celebratory, liberating, engaging, full of hope and expectation, affirming, restoring, free of distractions, thought provoking, and reflective—where individuals can meet with God (though it will not always be all of those things at once).

Our goal is not to *get people to worship corporately*, though certainly that happens in our environment. We believe we could not manipulate it if we tried—by nature of worship being an act of an individual's own will. We can only influence and create space conducive for it.

We believe verbiage such as "Let's begin our time of worship," though not inappropriate, has led people to define worship in a narrow and localized way. Language like this leads people to believe worship is an act associated with being in a "worship service" or at a church building. Unfortunately, this has also been perpetuated by the naming and designation of "praise and worship" music. In many cases, the corporate time of worship is gauged solely by the music, and the music is often referred to as the "worship."

But worship—biblically speaking—is a responsive way of living. It is more fabric, all encompassing, and global, not simply an act or strictly about music or any interactive vehicle we may design. Typically, church nomenclature has minimized and contextualized worship into acts largely revolving around music as well as other acts within the "worship service."

Our desire is to create an environment that has multiple layers that emerge and connect. We want some overlap at the seams of the layers so The Cue feels congruent, but enough independence to the layers that there are multiple themes people can grab (not inert ideas and exercises).

So then, as opposed to many models of corporate church gatherings, our goal is not simply one clear theme we are trying to drive home. A video for a story of a spiritual journey, a Top 40 song, or aesthetic design may or may not bring about a dovetailed thematic link, but the experience, fresh perspective, and collision with authentic life experience(s) make it all legitimate.

It is a time of aggregates and gateways. Moving forward. Asking questions. Dialogue. Facing hang-ups. Belonging before believing. Deconstructing religious (and not necessarily biblical) language and ruts. Understanding and being able to recognize beauty. Falling headlong into a Jesus love affair. These are all celebrated at The Cue. The Cue is an invitation to dialogue as much as it is a venue to respond—both live simultaneously and symbiotically. We are okay with tension and do not feel a need to "seal the deal" at the end of each 65-minute gathering.

We often are asked if we are a "seeker" church. The word "seeker" made its way into the church lexicon in the last fifteen years in no small part due to the great work of Willow Creek Church in South Barrington, Illinois. But since that time, what it means to design a "seeker service" has developed into a cornucopia of definitions, all coming with their own variety of criticism from different groups as Christians continue to waste time on the wrong battlefields and argue about methodology as a whole instead of examining their communities and developing their own personality and authentic responses.

We contend that "seekers," or not-yet believers or spiritually curious people, come in all shapes and sizes. Therefore, if seeker services are the goal, the immediate and obvious question should become, "Which seeker?" While we celebrate some of that early thinking regarding seeker services, our goal is not to design a seeker service of any variety.

Similarly, our goal is not to create an environment that separates believers from not-yet believers, waters down theology to make it more palatable, or caters to bottom-shelf or universalist spirituality (all things we have been accused of—mostly from people who have attended fewer than a couple of times or never at all). We believe Jesus is the Way, the Truth, and the Life—our only way to Father God. Our goal is not "worship evangelism" in the sense that we want people to see what we model and become like us. The people in The Cue are not our "projects." They are human beings, designed by their Creator to worship him. We want them to know him. We want to know him more.

Westwinds has found itself in the mainstream media as well as the blogosphere in large part because of The Cue. We're proud of the ways we innovate and create, but it didn't happen overnight. It has been a long road fostering a community that values imagination, permission, authenticity, and community. It's been a repetitive dialogue wherein we invite one another to collectively craft ways to make church a place our neighbors would want to come to.

The Cue and all of Westwinds's methodology is not an attempt at being "relevant," which is usually ghettoized to mean "look and speak cool." It's about incarnation and a particular offense to mediocrity.

147

More than that, it's a deep-rooted belief that God has called us to act upon the stuff in our heads. The thirst for the sacred, the mysteries of God, the magic of the sacraments, the other-worldliness of corporate worship, the tears spent on broken people—they call us to act. We act by creating. By making stuff. We incarnate our thoughts into visual art and music and poetry and film. Projects, proposals, and petitions. Moments and movements. The Cue is a main venue for this creativity.

The Cue exists to . . .
create an original, unsullied, experience-rich, multi-layered environment in which we increase the occurrence of people interacting with God, his Word, his truth, and his people, and face the barriers that interrupt and antagonize the life Jesus invites.

The only non-negotiable element in the whole Cue experience is God's Word as the living, enlightening torrent of truth that must be present every time. Other than that, everything else is negotiable.

This philosophy of The Cue means we can design the experience around any elements that are excellent and connect into biblical themes we feel are current needs or culturally vital.

The role of symbol, metaphor, and image are integral in designing The Cue. While not an absolute mandate, for each Cue series design we desire to "speak" through a central (or multiple) image, metaphor, or symbol to influence people's hearts, minds, and emotions with the big picture—just as Jesus did with the parables.

At Westwinds, we are committed to designing The Cue in ways that have never been implemented in the traditional church, even though innovation—in and of itself—is not the goal.

The argument over the use of secular music, movies, and art in church is a non-issue for us. We firmly believe in the much-used statement "All truth is God's truth." All art—secular and otherwise (though we resist such delineation)—has the potential to illuminate, bolster, and augment the truth of God's Word as well as create dialogue. This is a method of teaching and sharing that is not new to us but is prevalent in scripture and was used by Jesus, the Apostle Paul, and many others.

Furthermore, because art is not worship but rather is a vehicle through which we may worship or reflect or respond to God, we should not have an opportunity to confuse motive for using such art. If a song is "performed" in The Cue space, it should never be suspect as "non-worshipful." God's truth permeates art and culture, and often secular art is a more applicable and honest statement that can be used to surface a need to know, create discussion, set a mood, present a situation, resonate with a person's current circumstances, cause us to question, answer a question, provoke thought, and move a heart.

It has been a popular practice in churches over the past decade or so to take a prompt from the business world and clearly define the "target audience." This language is somewhat unpalatable to us, though we certainly understand why many think it is important. Churches that define target audiences are usually asking questions about who they are catering to, who is in their neighborhood, and how they should tailor their programs and messages to meet the particular needs of that group. In many ways, this is how businesses approach sales. Is my community interested in my product? How much are they willing to pay? How can I surface their need to buy? What are their particular needs, and how can my product meet that need . . . so they buy it?

At Westwinds, in relation to programs and The Cue, our approach is different in more ways than it is similar. We certainly would agree it is unwise to believe one model or device that works well in one demographic would work as well in another. For instance, drama may work just fine in South Barrington but may be a miserable failure in South Beach. Instead of asking "Who is our target audience?" we ask a different question based on who we are, our personalities and culture, our backgrounds, and the kind of bona fide creativity and thought patterns that flow from within. We ask, "Who will most likely be attracted to Westwinds?"

The *religious disenfranchised*, *the spiritually curious*, *the artist*, and *the intellectual* will most likely be attracted to Westwinds. That is who we are. It is safe to say many are thriving in our environment who would not readily place themselves in that category, but such is life. We are attracted to what we are attracted to. We celebrate this.

WHO IS WELCOME AT YOUR CHURCH?

"Come dirty" has become the operative advice when anyone asks questions about who is welcome at our church. "Can I wear jeans?" "I just went through a divorce." "I haven't been to church in years." "I don't know if I believe in God." "I am angry at God." None of these things should stand in the way of someone feeling welcome here.

Many already falsely believe they will be struck by lightning if they attend any church. We shouldn't drive this fear deeper by our response to people's *situations*, whatever they may be. We're all dirty without Jesus. We *cannot* forget this.

I recently received an email in our general information inbox from a young man who described himself as a "twenty-one-year-old Christian who is also gay." He very graciously told us he was having a hard time finding a church to attend and wanted to know our "stance on LGBT Christians attending our church," adding, "I look forward to any reply you choose to give."

Notice that his question was *not* about whether I believe being gay is a sin; it was about him being welcome here or not.

This was my reply to him:

> *Dear _____,*
>
> *Thanks for the email. I am one of the pastors on staff here.*
>
> *I would hope that Westwinds is always a place where anyone feels welcome—welcome to pursue God, welcome to worship, welcome to feel at home.*
>
> *We do have a few people who are gay attending and serving at Westwinds. I know because I have had many sit down talks with them where they have confided in me. I think all of them would say they feel welcome at Westwinds.*
>
> *I will admit that some have not felt welcome here and that hurts us. I think I know why and I will do my best to shed light on that. Please give me grace. Sometimes I fear answering this question in an email because I am afraid no matter what I say or how I say it—it has the possibility of coming out all wrong. I won't pretend to know any of the hurt and pain you must experience trying to find a place to call your own.*
>
> *Westwinds has a very strong stance that every human being regardless of sexual orientation, race, background, preference, personality, etc. should be given the same rights afforded to every human being. I hope and pray our congregation is loving, courteous,*

helpful, and respectful to everyone who comes through our doors. I believe most gay people who attend West-winds feel that love.

However, Westwinds does believe that sexuality is a biblical moral issue and as such we have many dif-fering opinions on how to engage the questions sur-rounding homosexuality. In other words, we never want anyone to feel like they aren't welcome if they are gay but then issues come up like "Would you marry a gay couple?" and we don't. This is where it has the potential to go bad. As far as we understand the Bible's teaching on homosexuality, we believe there are prohibitions.

We realize there are differing opinions. Despite our personal convictions, we never want our actions to be dismissive of anyone. I personally believe I have a responsibility to love and be in relationship with everyone regardless of what I believe, they believe, my hang-ups, disagreements, or differing opinions. But I also realize it is those things that have potential to drive wedges. So I pray I am fighting hard to love people as I would want them to love me.

We would not tolerate anyone being hostile toward the gay community. We do not want our people to be homophobic. But, because I want to be completely hon-est with you, you would have to be aware that while you are very welcome there is a theological issue we have wrestled with and our position on the issue is one that may not be popular with the gay community.

So, we encourage our people to seek to understand. We encourage them to know what they believe—rather than point the finger at someone who is gay and treat them harshly just because someone told them it was wrong. We encourage them to listen. We don't tolerate hatred.

I'm sure it's messy. I'm sure we have a lot to learn. We may have differing opinions but I hope they would never be reason for anyone to cast judgment or make anyone feel unwelcome.

Hope you will come to Westwinds and give it a shot. This is a great community of people.

Whether or not you take a similar stance on homosexuality is not the issue here. When asking the question "What do I already believe about church?" it is in these scenarios where the rubber meets the road. What you believe about church shapes the personality of your church and answers the question about who is welcome and who is not. I prayed over my response for a day and hit *send*. His response to me was very comforting.

John,

Thank you so much for your prompt and informative reply.

I thank you so much for your willingness to be open about your beliefs even though you fear they may not be the answer I was hoping to hear.

I will definitely visit sometime. I have a friend who attends and she also told me that I would feel welcome. Thank you for your honesty and thank you for your kind and careful answer. I really appreciate that very much.

My response to this young man came from a deep-seated belief that he matters to God. That he is not my project. That what I may or may not believe about sin does not change the fact that I do not believe I'm the one who convicts anyone of it.

153

Plumbline #24 Worship Is an Orientation, Not an Event

It is a posture, not a program. As such, music can be worship, performance can be worship, and work can be worship. The occurrence is incidental; the heart is what matters to God.

I would think this one would go without saying, but because we still find ourselves in so many conversations regarding everything from "What is the appropriate volume of music on the weekend?" to "Why did we sing that Johnny Cash song during the baptism?" it's worth mentioning in our plumblines.

It seems that most conversations surrounding worship are in the context of corporate worship *or* personal worship. We often separate the two but seldom talk about them happening congruently. What about our personal response to God in corporate settings? Worship is a heart matter. Whether you are in a group of people who have chosen the songs without your input, taking part in a short-term mission project you didn't organize, working for a boss who tells you what to do or not do, or sitting on your deck at home with your Bible and favorite worship tunes, worship is about how you respond to God.

Years ago (and I can't remember where), I read that a popular rock star said he feels just as at home in the back of a Buddhist temple as he does in his church at home. Some Christians went crazy and condemned him for this statement. But what I understand him to say is that he could respond to God in whatever situation he was placed in. Worship is not conditional upon what is fed to us or is happening around us. This doesn't mean we don't have a responsibility to foster an environment conducive to people encountering God in meaningful and transformational ways. But it does mean that people will have varying opinions of what should go into that mix.

Quirky leaders must understand they have the permission to create an environment for corporate worship based upon personal taste, cultural exegesis, community story, situations, and their own unique context without apology. They invite the Holy Spirit to speak into every mundane, profane, and insane minute of their church's life, ask for help in interpreting the narrative around them, look for God in everything, and do their best to create an environment in which the people respond to all that God has revealed Himself to be in the ways that are unique to that community. The rest is up to the individual and God.

Sometimes the elements of our worship gatherings and the space we worship in have been written off as quirks:

We like our music loud.

The room is dark.

We move the stage area around a lot.

We change up the room aesthetic constantly.

We use PG-13 language.

We have a lot of abstract art around.

But all these things are decisions we have made through exegeting our own culture. The majority of people like all these things about us. They ring true. Some simply tolerate a couple of things on the list. I have a special love for the ones who quietly tolerate, engage, and respond regardless of personal preference in one or two areas.

Plumbline #25 Theology Is Playful. Orthodoxy Is Absolute.

We never mess with the core doctrines. Ever. We stand in line with thousands of years of Christian history and tradition, but we also recognize that there is room for imaginative re-renderings of biblical concepts, characters, and context within the boundaries of orthodoxy, especially as it serves to help others better understand the Story of God and the World.

Rob Bell wrote a great book called *Velvet Elvis* that speaks to this plumbline. In it, he describes himself as part of a long tradition marked by people like Martin Luther who stood up and said, "Is that really what scripture says?" and challenged conventional understandings of what it means to be a Christian. He talks about the idea of leaders having to reform constantly:

> By this I do not mean cosmetic, superficial changes like better lights and music, sharper graphics, and new methods with easy-to-follow steps. I mean theology; the beliefs about God, Jesus, the Bible, salvation, the future. We must keep reforming the way the Christian faith is defined, lived, and explained.

I remember having a conversation with Cheryll a few years ago at my kitchen table. She had a hundred unanswered questions that kept her from making a decision to follow Jesus. "Was the world really created in six days and God needed to take a breather?" "What do we do about the dinosaurs?" "Why aren't women allowed to serve in some churches?" "How do I understand what God's 'will' is?" "Was Jesus ever married?" All good questions. But not the ones that really matter.

I told Cheryll that if we wrote all her questions down, they would fill the whole kitchen table. But the questions that mattered to her becoming a Jesus follower or not would fit on a very small napkin on that table. Questions like, "Who is Jesus?" "Why do I need him?" "Do I believe who he said he is?" These are the questions that matter. We can't fool around with these answers and call ourselves Christians. Your answers to these questions align you with Jesus, or not.

I told Cheryll about the thief on the cross. We read the story in Luke 23. I asked her, "What did the thief know?"

"He just knew who Jesus was and that he needed him." Bingo.

Cheryll then joined our satellite group, and we wrestled with questions for the next few years. She gave her life to Jesus. Without the majority of those questions settled.

We are okay with tension. We entertain questions. We believe questions are part of faith. We believe mystery and paradox are inherent in the Christian faith. We don't believe Christianity is about solving every mystery and having an answer for every question or situation. The mysteries drive us to more questions. We celebrate and entertain them all in light of the person of Jesus.

This sometimes makes people fidgety. When we don't speak in black and white terms on issues that aren't even addressed in scripture, they sometimes draw conclusions that we don't have integrity because we aren't willing to make a stand.

That isn't true. We make a stand every day. For Jesus. We just choose not to stand *against* the things we think he doesn't care about or the things we believe may not get resolved in our lifetime. Or anyone else's.

(For some more helpful thoughts on this, visit David's blog at shadowinggod.com and search the phrase "theology and math.")

SOMEONE WILL ALWAYS THINK YOUR CHURCH SUCKS

There are a lot of churches and church models to choose from. Is it the liturgical church or the *relevant* one? House church or megachurch? Mainline or rebellious dissenter? The truth is, expressions of church vary. That's not a bad thing. What's bad is that some are led to believe the right recipe for his or her church has already been successfully crafted by *another* and exists *out there*.

In reality, you have to find out what God is saying to *you* about the *particular franchise* of church *you* are called to lead. It is imperative to surface what you believe about how things get done, how you engage the world around you, how people grow, the role of public worship, who is welcome, day-to-day business, leadership roles, and what your voice is in the community in which you live in the context of your expression.

The quirky leader's role is not to pick a style of church off the menu that is least offensive and most appealing to his or her imaginary guests who may or may not show up at the table. The role pleads for the discerning of one's own palate, being familiar with the local crops, bartering with local merchants, and creating a feast that celebrates the individual's culinary genius. You, the quirky leader, must stand behind what is being served. When you are approached by someone who thinks your cuisine is detestable or needs to be changed, you need to be able to say, "I'm sorry it's not to your liking. This is what we serve here. And we're darn good at it. It's local, home-grown, prepared by our own chefs, and our regular clientele find it amazing."

CHAPTER SEVEN:
LIFE IN REAL LIFE

*Life is what happens to you while you're busy
making other plans.*

—John Lennon

We could easily replace the word *life* in the above quotation with *leadership*.

Leadership life experience counts. While it is important that leaders continually stay sharp and allow ourselves to be challenged by new ideas about leadership, it is equally or more important that we learn from our past. Leaders must embrace their past to shape their future.

Likewise, we have to learn from our present. We have to be note-takers. While we plan and innovate and strategize, we need to listen to what the Spirit is speaking. What our friends are speaking. What our spouses are speaking. What our editors are speaking.

While I wouldn't necessarily subscribe to the notion that "everything happens for a reason" (when that phrase is translated as if God *orchestrates* disasters to teach us lessons), I believe God wants to redeem every failure, misstep, hurt, and ministry catastrophe we've experienced.

Leaders need to use their lifelong leadership experience and practice leadership hermeneutics (observing, interpreting, and applying) to exegete their own leadership principles. Our best lessons are learned by paying attention in the middle of chaos and evaluating our experiences on the other side. While books, seminars, podcasts, and the like can certainly speak into our experience and help us evaluate where we want to go next, we need to develop a rubric for evaluating where we are now and where we have come from.

THIS ALL SOUNDS FINE AND DANDY

My wife and I were sitting with our friend Kim and her husband recently in a coffee shop. She's in ministry too. They have a different church style than ours but have had a lot of the same challenges over the years. We were talking through leadership principles (some of the very ones in this book), and she hit the pause button. She told me it was very cool I was writing this book to encourage leaders to give themselves permission to ask, "Who said you can't do ministry that way?" and applauded many of the things I was saying about finding your own voice and charting new courses. Then she said, "But what do you do when you aren't the person at the top and will never be?"

Kim, the first part of this chapter is for you, and for all the Kims out there. Finding your own voice, celebrating your quirks, and defining principles and plumblines is not just for the person who signs the paychecks. While the person with the reins does own the ultimate responsibility for laying down the law, developing plumblines is about communication, understanding, and the way you lead yourself as much as it is about how you call the shots for others.

If you are a leader in a ministry situation who works under another leader who doesn't see things eye to eye with you, you have two choices: submit or move on.

Before you get a picture in your mind of me condoning a ministry leader forced to walk ten paces behind who bows to the every whim of a tyrant leader, take a breath. Some situations are unhealthy. Like in any relationship.

Too many church leaders, however, are quick to flee these days. We too readily allow ourselves to spiritualize and re-label our own hurts, conflicts, preferences, and visions of greener pastures to justify moving on when the going gets rough. Don't get me wrong; there are good times to move on in ministry. And in those situations, there are right and wrong ways to move on. Unfortunately, there's a whole lot of messiness with parting ways these days.

Church leaders are really good about preaching that life doesn't always go as planned. We give marital advice about sticking it out and commitment. We talk about the benefits of longevity and conflict resolution with people we counsel. Then, when someone in a leadership position above us doesn't let us express our inner butterfly, we shout, "Kill the beast!"

I know all the Kims might think it's easy for me to say because I am the guy at the top in my current scenario (not *you*, Kim—the other Kims). But the only reason I can say these things with absolute assurance is that I haven't always been. Most of my ministry experience has been working *for* someone else.

In California, Brad was my boss for years. We disagreed on a horde of things and had oceans of differences in our personalities. (Disclaimer: Our differences were not always a black and white, polar extreme dichotomy. I don't want Brad to sound square or uninteresting.) Brad hated tension. I lived in it. Brad didn't really care for art. I am an artist and love art. Brad liked to worship in bright spaces. I like to manipulate the light. Brad wore slacks. I wear jeans. Brad is clean shaven. I am not, and I view my facial hair like some view their garden or hedges. Brad was a big fan of small groups. I could live with them or without them. Brad loved the old hymns. I liked to play with a lot of variety, but mostly rock and roll. Brad liked to hear people singing in the room. I thought it should be loud enough that people don't hear singing next to them and feel free to sing loud. Often, Brad thought my ideas were too extreme. I thought his were too corporate. This list could go on all day.

One day, about twenty years ago, I called Brad to ask him a question. He didn't answer the phone right away (we didn't have caller ID back then, or I'm sure he would have dropped everything for me). After a few tries, Brad picked up the phone. We chatted for a couple of minutes, and then he asked me if it was super important that we talk right then. Apparently, I called during the last game of the World Series. I wasn't even aware it was baseball season. I was watching *Jeopardy!* when I called.

There were rules of the road I had to submit to under Brad's leadership. While there was freedom to disagree on any number of things, at the end of the day Brad had the final say. Because I too believed in Brad's overall vision, I had to understand that some of my crazy schemes might not come to fruition under his leadership because they did not fit.

So how does a creative person who is also a leader of sorts with a penchant for crazy ideas and an affinity for coloring outside the lines survive in an environment where he feels he can't exercise all those muscles? What do you do when you answer to someone who is cut from an entirely different cloth?

I'm a fan of Top Ten lists, so here you go.

1. Start with your quirks.

This process still counts. Do not underestimate the power of identifying your own quirks and defining your own plumblines, no matter what level you are at in any hierarchy. This process not only helps you know yourself better, but it also helps you to say what you want to say succinctly and not sound like a rambling idiot. Quirk-flavored plans can sound like inert ideas to someone who doesn't understand your own inner big picture. Help them see it.

2. Define the rules of engagement.

Knowing how to fight in a church staff structure is much like in a marriage. There are some places in which you should not fight. There are some people you should not disagree in front of. There are things you should never say. You can't use the Bible or the past as a weapon. There are times of day that are too stressful for creative solutions to surface. Communicate with your leader about what he or she needs to fight fair. You do the same. Stick to those rules.

3. Learn how to rhyme.

Sometimes, you won't get to do your thing. But don't put your thing out to pasture. Reshape it. Reinvent it. Put your ideas to work in ways that rhyme with the big vision. Be inventive. Cast your vision to your leader and show how your particular bent is good beyond your particular axe to grind.

Rhyming is like the art of *mixed media*. This art form combines various distinct traditional visual art media in one piece of art. For example, a mixed media oil painting may incorporate text, found objects, and photography. The end result is something beautiful that feels right and true. Often, artists will collaborate on projects in which there is a mutual trust that the end result will be a rhyming of their individual media.

Rhyming is like songwriting. In Nashville, there is a saying: "Change a word, get a third." When a songwriter pens a song, he or she often will get input from other sources, such as fellow songwriters or producers. Sometimes songs are changed significantly for the better by simple additions or subtractions. When this happens, the collaborator takes part in the spoils. The collaborator sees the value in his or her addition and doesn't feel slighted because he or she didn't get to rewrite the whole song. The song's integrity matters most.

4. Use your inside voice.

Sometimes it seems your ideas should not be put aside. They are too good. And yet you find yourself butting heads with your leader. In those instances, if the idea really matters, ask your leader how you can pursue your idea(s) without conflict or the appearance of insubordination.

In many cases, your leader wants you to be able to pursue your ideas in a different fashion. Under different circumstances. Your voice matters, but it's not your place to scream louder.

For years, Brad and I had different ideas about corporate worship. It wasn't necessarily that Brad thought my ideas were bad or inappropriate; they just didn't line up with his vision for Sunday morning. But Brad and I worked out ways to let me experiment with some of those ideas in other contexts. We had occasional midweek gatherings and evening gatherings where Brad allowed me to craft something different. Brad encouraged me to be involved with city organizations where my particular flavor was needed. We hosted house concerts and parties where we tried some things on for size.

Many times, leaders and subordinate leaders argue too strongly over the value of A versus B without entertaining the idea of a possible C that's waiting to be discovered. Often, C might be a very attractive option to both of you. If C cannot be found within the boundaries of the mission, ruminate about how it might be possible to accomplish A or B in another aspect of life or ministry.

5. Remember, you're not *that awesome*.

One of my favorite shows to watch these days is a television series called *Suits*. The setting for the show is a fictitious law firm in New York. The characters are well written: witty, sarcastic, funny, and smart. But they are painfully self-absorbed. Part of what makes the show so entertaining is anticipating who is going to self-destruct next. It's a hyperbolic look at a workplace where everyone tries to one up everyone else. Unfortunately, it reminds me of some church staffs.

In a Season 2 episode, one of the leaders tells his intern, "When I was in your position, I thought I was smarter than everyone else and had better ideas. I was. And I did. But it wasn't my time" (my paraphrase).

We all have a small part of us that thinks we can do things better. If we didn't, we wouldn't lead. But the church shouldn't work like *Suits*. Jesus reminds us on plenty of occasions that we should not think too highly of ourselves, and pretty much all sin boils down to pride. That's where it all started to go bad.

When our need to dominate and prove how awesome we are eclipses the mission, we are out of line. Check your motives.

Oh, and a thousand people want your job. Today. Believe it or not, some of them can actually do it.

6. Is it a big thing or a little thing?

This question has saved my marriage. And my relationship with my kids. And it has kept my children from murdering one another at times. It's simple. Is this *thing* worth going to the mat for? Sometimes it is. Most of the time, it isn't. If you constantly find yourself in conflict situations where it becomes impossible for you to bend or decipher between big and little things, it may be time to move on. But not in a self-righteous pouting kind of a way. Don't be dumb.

7. Ask yourself, "Would Apple allow this?"

I am always amazed at how some church employees act as if it is their God-given right to challenge everything that leadership hands down. Somewhere along the line, some church staff people came to the conclusion that it is their moral obligation to question authority. Perhaps it is because the seeds of defiance and division were never addressed when they were shouting from the pews.

✳ The fact is, there is no company in corporate America that would allow even close to the level of defiance and insubordination that happens every day in churches. It is leadership's problem for letting it happen as much as it is the staff members' problem for their elevated view of the role they play.

What company would allow any staff person to operate under the "better to get forgiveness than permission" rule? What CEO would allow his employees to change the branding of his or her company simply because they got a wild streak of creativity? It wouldn't happen. But it happens in our churches.

If you want to pick a fight with the good men and women who lead you and make decisions in what they feel is the best interest of your church, check your tone, pace your gait, examine your motives, and ask if your attitude and stance would be tolerated anywhere else outside the church.

8. Play as if you are a part of the band.

On any given Sunday, we have at least five musicians on stage. Whenever we start practicing a song, it sounds horrible. It's not that the musicians don't know their parts or that they don't play the right notes. It's that it takes a few run-throughs to play those parts *as a band*. At first shot, everyone is a soloist. Fighting to be heard. Checking their monitors.

Massaging a song and making it sound good is a process of learning not to play as much as it is learning how to play. Sometimes, the drummer has to remember the song is not all about how hard he or she hits the drums. The singers have to blend instead of sounding like two or three soloists in a cage fight.

What part do you play? Play it well. That means you have to listen as well as finesse your own skill at your particular instrument.

9. Quit whining about passion.

Creative leaders are notorious for shouting about how they are being deprived of following and developing their passions. But they aren't the only ones. I know leaders who don't have a creative bone in their body but carry the banner of "Everything rises and falls on leadership" with a militant passion.

Obviously, I'm a fan of creativity. Individuality. No one wants anyone to have a spiritual superiority complex, as warned against in 1 Corinthians 12. Everyone has a place, and all should be able to find theirs in the kingdom economy. I believe in finding what you love to do and finding a way to get paid for it. Be all you can be. Reach for the stars. Yada, yada, yada.

But . . .

Tell me where Jesus said the pursuit of our passions is paramount in everything. Do a study of passion in the Bible and see what following it does.

I was horrible and wrong about passion early in my ministry. Horribly wrong. My "No one puts baby in a corner" approach to ministry was sinful. We need to think about our wording in our blog posts and what we are preaching when it comes to following our passion.

An uncomfortable number of ministry leaders are about two clicks to the left on their passion intensity knob. This makes them vulnerable to experiencing the deep, disturbing results of following one's passion when it is unbridled. In the name of passion, art often turns ugly, relationships go south, and ministries crumble.

10. Invite the Spirit.

One of the best things Brad and I ever did when we worked on the same staff was read together. A host of voices can speak into your very situation without you having to be a wordsmith. Brad and I would often encourage each other to read a book and give honest feedback or pick a book and read it together as a conversation starter (we still do this across the country from one another).

Reading together was just one of the ways we invited the Spirit into our everyday activity and gave Him room to speak. Visiting other churches, meeting with other pastors and leaders, meeting with no agenda but to pray, road trips, and listening to each other's music invited interruption and provided room for a voice other than our own.

Give the Spirit permission. You may find he changes your mind sometimes. Or the other person's. Or both of yours.

11. Expand your own horizons.

I know I said Top Ten, but consider this a bonus (or a quirk?).

Often, we don't realize how conditioned we are to feel a certain way because of the environment we live in and the people we choose to listen to. This is why Bruce Springsteen is the patron saint of New Jersey. There is a group of people who would fight to the death in honor of The Boss. His story is their story. But for a kid growing up in Detroit, MI, Springsteen will be totally irrelevant in light of Eminem's influence.

No one in an image-rich, media-drenched, developed world hones his or her tastes in isolation. In the church, we are influenced by denominations, favored authors of our tribe, popular conferences, any manner of Christian subculture, and the world we exist in.

Because of this, every February I read only fiction (February is not particularly special, but it starts with "F" like fiction, and the alliteration reminds me). From varying genres. I find if I read only books on theology, church leadership, etc., I become uninventive and unproductive. In similar fashion, I challenge myself to listen to music I don't always gravitate toward. I sometimes let David pick movies even though I think I will hate them. And my favorite restaurant is the one I haven't been to yet.

By doing this, I've expanded my horizons and developed new tastes. Sometimes in dramatic fashion. Encourage your leader(s) to commit to a pursuit of understanding and expanding your palates (or palettes, whichever you prefer).

Brad and I finally did part ways a few years back. Only as fellow staffers. He's one of my best friends. He's got my back. Likewise, I'd attempt to fight Lady Gaga in a cage match to defend him. Last summer, Brad called and invited me to participate in Lakeside's 25th Anniversary Celebration. "It wouldn't be the same without you," he said. I cried.

I once heard it said, "The church you now belong to is the church you will be from one day." That may be true. Probably is for most of us. In some cases, a parting of the ways is healthy. Just do yourself a favor and ask yourself the following questions:

- Is God calling me *to* something else? (It's hard to make a case for God calling us away from anything unless there is somewhere to go).

- How is my attitude? Have I made enemies I need to get right with?

- Have I done everything I know to do to make things work?

- If God jumped in my face and told me to stay, would I?

- Is my decision kingdom motivated or me motivated? In other words, is this about saying yes to a bigger yes or just proving my point? Are Jesus and the church better served by my parting?

- Am I leaving in such a way that I will be welcomed back with open arms? What will they say about me when I'm gone?

- Have I sought wise counsel? Have I made this decision in isolation?

- What does my family think about my possible leaving? Will I trade one bit of drama for another?

- In what possible ways could my leaving damage the kingdom, the name of Jesus, or this particular franchise of the church? What do I have to do to prevent that from happening to the best of my ability?

- Have I poisoned anyone on the way out? Do I need to come clean? Often, we patch things up with those close to us and forget about the wake of opinion we left behind us.

- Is it possible I have something to learn in the thick of this I haven't left room for?

- If I stay, what is the worst possible thing that will happen? Will I be the only one who feels the uncomfortable effects of staying, and is it possible I could stay and get to *the other side* of this conflict, whatever that may be?

- If I were to rewrite the entire story of my season in this particular ministry, what would I do differently, and what changes would I make in my own heart? Is it too late to make those changes?

- Is it possible there is another end to this story with a more favorable outcome for everyone involved?

- Has God given me a particular prophetic voice that cannot be heard in this context, and is he moving me to a place where I can use that voice? Is it possible he wants me to be an agent of change in this environment?

EYES ON THE PRIZE

This is probably a good time to admit (as you've already walked the road of seven chapters) that I don't think I have a corner on the leadership market. I'd probably fail at many versions of standardized leadership tests.

I don't think I have fully matured as a leader by any means. You probably feel the same. But we can't let those feelings of inadequacy stagnate us. The biblical idea of maturity is, in part, knowing that we will never be fully mature in this life. Our eyes stay on the goal while we run the race—dropping our batons occasionally.

And what is the goal? Good leadership, right?

Hell, no.

As in, that is a lie from the pit of hell. No.

The goal is Jesus. Period.

"What is life teaching me about leadership?" (while it is not a *bad* question) is not the most honorable question we can ask. The way we ask questions sometimes gets us more useful answers. Maybe, "What is Jesus saying to me and my people through this?" is better. "How does God want me to help navigate through this landscape?" "How do I elevate Jesus through this?" "How do I surface people's need to pay attention to Jesus in the middle of this?" "How am I falling more in love with Jesus as I lead, and how can I translate that story to others in order to help them?"

When we ask questions like these, in light of Jesus in us and others, we remind ourselves the world doesn't revolve around us. If our identity is in our leadership, we are in for a world of hurt. Our deepest identity, who we are at the very core, is not leaders. We are Jesus' people.

When we see ourselves as Jesus followers, on the same journey as the people we are called to lead, we do ourselves a great favor. We don't set ourselves up for failure because we should *know better.* When we see ourselves as fellow sojourners and talk in these terms, we allow our people to see us as guides rather than gurus, teachers rather than sages, and people ready to take bullets for the team instead of yelling at everyone to tell them where to point and shoot while we retreat to a safe spot in the back of the battle lines.

LEADERSHIP LESSONS FROM MALACHI

We don't know a lot about Malachi. In fact, outside of the book of Malachi, we know nothing. As a matter of fact, we don't really know that "Malachi" was someone's name. Malachi translated means "messenger," or perhaps even "His Messenger."

While who wrote the book of Malachi is a question nobody really knows the answer to, the book's validity, congruency, importance, authority, and potency have never been questioned. Parts of the book of Malachi are quoted in the Second Testament by Jesus himself.

The Messenger, in the tradition of the First Testament prophets, doesn't mince his words. In fact, some of the harshest words in the Bible against God's people can be found in this book.

Malachi is the last in the line of First Testament prophets. Haggai and Zechariah preached during the rebuilding of the temple in Jerusalem after the Babylonian exile. In Malachi, the temple is finished, and the worship there has already become monotonous and mechanical for the people.

The Messenger in any age is not always popular. The world likes its Jesus looking like a Chippendale's dancer, knocking on doors with a smile, and holding little lambs. No one wants to see him kicking tail. But he's both a loving and gentle friend and a demanding judge. He makes no apologies for that, and we shouldn't either.

Malachi's audience was paralyzed. Forgetful. Apathetic. Stupid. Complacent. Just like me at times. And just like you. The Messenger says, *It's high time to call things what they are.*

172

Malachi begins with a little history lesson to remind God's people of how ultimately he has protected and preserved them throughout history. To remind them of his faithful love. Were they disciplined along the way? Heck yeah. That's part of his love. Did they encounter pain and suffering? A ton. But here they are, in a time of peace, nothing prompting them to fall on their knees. Nothing causing them to cry out. They had forgotten.

God said, "I love you." And, they said, "Really? How have you loved us?"

I keep notes and I blog to remind myself of what God has done and what he is doing because I am stupid. I am forgetful. I'm self-absorbed. God says, "I love you." And I say, "Really? How have you loved me?" I need the stories. The stories are my lifeline.

READ THE SHORT BOOK OF MALACHI ONLINE AT COMMON ENGLISH BIBLE.COM

We don't want to say it out loud, but if we're honest, it's in the difficult times that we feel closest to God. The times when we are talking to God minute by minute, waiting for deliverance, waiting for hope, waiting for help . . . and when it comes, we celebrate. Then we forget. Quite easily.

When times are peaceful, it's easy for us to forget our source of strength.

Malachi interrupts the time of peace. Stirs it up. Their worship was shoddy. Their response to God was weak. They weren't giving God the best. As a matter of fact, they were quite literally giving God the worst.

At the time of Malachi, the temple sacrificial system was in order. People brought animals to the temple to be sacrificed by the priests on their behalf because of their sin. Every time that perfect animal was sacrificed, they were supposed to feel the pain. The shame. So they would turn. It was horrid—to go through the hassle and the pain of bringing innocent sacrifices because of their sin.

They were taking the animals that were going to die anyway, or the ones that were useless to them, and giving them to God. God was not happy. Their particular sacrifices cost them nothing.

God said, "Why don't you just shut the doors of the temple?" You've missed the point. Your worship costs you nothing. You show up and do your duty. Whatever that is. It doesn't please me. Might as well stay home.

To drive his point further home, God tells the priests he wants to rub their faces in the offal of their festival sacrifices (the internal waste of the sacrifices usually carried outside the camp) and have them be carried outside of the town as well.

Some of the stuff the Messenger was calling into question was blatant, hurtful, damaging sin. In Chapter 2, we learn these idiots were trading in their old wives for newer versions. These same guys were crying out before God and asking, "Why aren't you blessing us?" God says (my paraphrase), "I'll tell you why. I am standing here as a witness to your crimes. You have ditched the wife of your youth. Remember the one you fell in love with when you were younger? You were younger too, but somehow you forgot that. Now you're divorcing them and messing around on IsraeliMatch.com."

Some of their sin was apathy. Non-urgency. Complaining. Not looking after the folks they should have been taking care of. Not being hospitable. Not taking care of the poor and defenseless. They were comfortable. And complacent.

Picture your leadership life as a car. When you were first being rolled out on the showroom floor, you had lots of potential. People noticed you. You showed everyone your killer dashboard, gadgets, flashing lights, state-of-the-art sound system. You dreamed of all the places you would go.

You took the car out for a spin. Went on a cross-country trip. Took the top down and felt the breeze. Picked up hitchhikers. Carpooled. Got groceries. You did all the stuff a car is supposed to do.

But over time, some of us get caught up in the gadgets. The killer stereo. The comfortable seats. Some of us sit and read the manual. And we forget the main purpose of the car: to move.

So we park it. And we enjoy the gadgets. The comfort.

What does it take to get us going? Someone rear-ending us? An emergency call that requires we get across town? Someone walking by and catching the young hussy we have in the backseat?

Thomas Merton said, "The spiritual life is first of all life." It's not something we merely talk about or think about or study; we live it. We invest in it. We invest financially, mentally, emotionally, spiritually, and physically.

We don't simply WILL ourselves to change and to deepen in our spiritual lives. Our wills only get us so far. They are like our car battery. If our cars ran only on our batteries, we wouldn't get far at all.

The metaphor of "bearing spiritual fruit" is a good one for us to remember. Fruit doesn't just exist. It isn't willed into existence. Love, joy, peace, patience—we don't just *decide* to exhibit these things. They are things that flow out of a rich life source. If you are an angry person and you say, "That's it; I will now be kind," good luck. It doesn't happen that way. It comes with multiple tiny submissions to God. It comes with accountability. It comes with changing habits and adopting new ones. It comes with time. It often comes with pain.

In the last few verses of the book of Malachi, God tells us through the Messenger the kind of life he wants to give us: **"But for you who revere my name, the sun of righteousness will rise with healing in its wings. And you will go out and leap like calves released from the stall."**

We used to have goats growing up. They were hilarious when you let them free. Kicking up their heels, you'd think they were going to snap in half.

Do you remember that feeling? Where did it go?

Have you never experienced it? What's wrong?

PAYING YOUR LESSONS FORWARD

Unfortunately, our haunting past experiences often paralyze us. We don't want to repeat the same mistakes. And so many of us have stopped dreaming, innovating, risking. We may have paid some lessons forward, but only in that we fine-tune the same things over and over until they run smoothly and we feel good about ourselves and our leadership. Then we rest.

If the goal is Jesus, we can't rest.

The world isn't resting.

Because the world is not at rest, it presents new problems and challenges and opportunities every day. The quirky leader has to learn from experience but then draw out his or her future plans on an Etch-A-Sketch. When those plans stop working, shake the thing. Start again.

Ultimately, quirky leadership is more about faith than sight. While it has become quite popular to plan the future purposefully down to every last detail, quirky leadership is okay with taking it as it comes. Ready, fire, aim.

This doesn't mean we shouldn't have a good idea of where we want to go. It doesn't mean we throw common sense, time, money, and contrary opinion down the drain in some existential experiment to create ministry nirvana. It just means that usually by the time we think we have all the bugs worked out, everyone is tired of talking about it, we've sucked the fun out of the adventure, and we *still* get blindsided by things we didn't plan for, if we choose to embark on the adventure at all.

A few years ago, I bought a mountain bike. I love to take it out on trails and explore places I've never been. But I don't always get to ride it in the way it was intended. Most of the time, I ride on paved paths with my family. We take it slow. We go from one quaint town to another on the coast of Lake Michigan. My family is always telling me to slow down and not get too far ahead. For my wife and daughter, biking is about fresh air, transportation, family time, and occasionally exercise. I love these times with my family, but I have to change my mountain bike expectations.

The allure of the mountain bike is dirt, mud, sand, off-road adventure, uncharted territory, speed, and surprise. There is no greater mountain bike thrill for me than to speed down a mountain on a single-track path. Never knowing if it will have a drop-off or a stump in the way, having to pick up the bike and carry it across creeks and rivers, working up a sweat and working every one of those gears over varied terrain.

The rewards are much different on the mountain bike than on the paved path. It's not that the paved path doesn't have any rewards at all, but it's safe and predictable for the most part.

Mountain bike riding on a single-track path cannot be completely planned out beforehand. You can know where you are headed and you can ask other people about the route if they have traveled it before you, but it requires the ability to act and react. The rider is constantly looking ahead to choose his or her path. Once you're in it, the only thing you have to rely on is your balance and wisdom and agility from going down similar paths.

Your skill set is not based on going down the same path over and over, but rather on going down paths that have similar obstacles. When you travel off-road, the lines are always different. And those lines aren't always something you follow; sometimes you make new lines.

When I first got my bike, I got a third-degree separation in my left shoulder within a week. Ripped the ligaments right off. My clavicle looks like I have a huge bump to the left of my neck. It's not raised, but everything just hangs from it. It was painful when it happened. Still is.

I told the story in great detail to my mountain bike friends the week it happened. We laughed. They called me stupid in jest. We looked at the photos my friend took of me all bloodied up and crying.

My friend Jeff shook his head at me, smiled, and said, "No guts, no story."

This phrase has now become one of my leadership mottos. We all learned a lesson about what not to do when mountain biking. I took a beating. But it didn't make me or my friends not want to ride anymore. Quite the opposite. Mountain biking is not just about the thrill. It's about the *stories*. It's about what happens along the way. It's about seeing what no one else gets to see when they stay on the pavement and sharing that experience with others on the ride.

LESSONS FROM REALITY

I enjoy food competitions. *Cake Boss, Ace of Cakes, Chopped, Next Food Network Star*, you name it. If there is culinary art to be made and a palate to be impressed, I'm in.

One of the things I've noticed about cake competitions is how they build on lessons they learned from making the last cake. When so-and-so is hired to make a Leaning Tower of Pisa cake, it is not unusual for him to use the same methods of construction as in his Flying V Guitar cake. But no matter what lesson he learns from his leaning-tower cake, no one wants to watch him make it again. And again. We don't mind lessons being applied to new challenges, but who wants to see the perfect leaning-tower cake being made over and over?

We certainly wouldn't call the master of the leaning-tower cake a cake leader. While his first cake was amazing, the grandeur loses its allure by the second or third go-around. Pretty soon, no one cares about a leaning-tower cake. His niche is short-lived. He isn't paying attention to what is happening around him if he just keeps making the same cake. There are different cake demands out there. No one wants to watch Pisa cake again (that little play on words happened by accident, and I am so proud of myself right now).

Your people need answers to new challenges. Your people need you to create new challenges. Your people want you to help them be part of the process of creating good cakes for great occasions.

I'm also addicted to decorating shows. My wife watches them even more than I do. One particular favorite is called *Next Design Star*. This show presents designers with incredible challenges of defining space in hopes of getting their own reality show at the end of the competition.

In one recent season, a contestant made an incredible wall design for a room. The judges were impressed and gave her a lot of accolades. In the next room, which provided much different challenges, she ignored most of the things that should have been addressed (and that she could have easily addressed) to focus on a wall design. When it came time for the judges' reaction, they hated her room. They chided her for spending so much time on the wall design.

Confused and bewildered, she went into the next challenge with a militant desire to recapture the former glory she had in the first challenge. Her strategy was to find out where her wall design went wrong and correct it in the new landscape.

By the third time of seeing wall design become the focus for this designer, everyone was ready for her to go home. But the judges gave her one more chance because they knew she had something in her. They made their point clear: "Your wall design will not save you next round."

For some leaders, an outdated and ineffective program has become their Pisa cake. For some, their weekend service has become a wall design that no one pays any attention to any longer.

While experience counts, it counts only as much as you are willing to reshape your lessons in different applications or, better yet, allow your lessons to reshape you.

It's Not Funny

When a comedian writes a good joke, it should be told. But pretty soon, after that joke is told a thousand times, it loses impact. This is one of the reasons why my generation generally thinks Bob Hope wasn't funny at all. His jokes had the same style of delivery over and over, and he often told the same jokes.

Bob had another point of disconnect with us—we didn't understand him. He spoke a different language. He spoke a language he learned as a Vaudevillian and fostered during the Depression, one that barely survived the Vietnam years. Eventually, Bob was adored not because he was funny or relevant but because he was cute—in the same way your grandpa is cute when he tells the same joke to all your friends over and over.

While Bob certainly made his mark, he eventually lost his audience. The people who understood him died all around him. Their kids and grandkids weren't let in on the secrets that made him so appealing at one time.

Quirks and plumblines and life lessons need to be interpreted and exercised in context. To be inattentive to the context in which you are placed is to put yourself in danger of becoming a one-trick pony. Or, a joke.

Becky works part-time at Westwinds and is on staff at a local university. Recently, we talked about the challenges young people face moving from academia to real-world settings. In an effort to help students navigate this change and put their skills to the test, Becky runs a program that requires potential graduates in various programs to secure a contract with a paying company or individual for a project the student designs. Students shop themselves to a list of potential clients, make a pitch, secure a contract, and get a pass or fail grade depending on the success of that project (based on the hiring party's feedback).

One of the hurdles for students entering the real world of business is the task of understanding their client and surfacing their client's particular needs. Becky also teaches communication and public address courses in which *knowing your audience* is the number one rule. Becky described how painful it is to watch a student take book learning from various courses and try to apply it straight across the board in every situation, not realizing every business situation is unique. The task for Becky as a professor is to help these students understand their own quirks, find their own voice, and learn how to communicate with their clients and give the clients what they need.

Sometimes, the student sacrifices personal taste in the process. Students find, on many projects, they can't give the clients exactly what they want and they aren't the right person for the job. They often are hit with the reality that not everyone thinks they are superstars. Even when they're really good at what they do. In these cases, students start to learn what kind of businesses they can tailor their skills to, or they start to develop other skills to help them meet real needs without sacrificing their voices in the process. They learn to decide what is worth fighting for and what isn't.

As children, we begin learning in environments where we are told to spit back exactly what we're told or what we read in order to get a passing grade. Sometimes we're lucky enough to have teachers along the way who equip us with tools that put us on a path of self-discovery, reason, expression, and the ability to form our own thoughts.

Even then, we're given grades based on our ability to define and articulate our position on our own merit. In the real world, those *thus sayeth me* ideals we possessed as a carefree and independent student are challenged and poked at as we put them into action. We need to learn to adapt our ideals to context, people, learning styles, desires, needs, situations, problems, conflicts, vision, mission, and job descriptions that aren't of our own choosing, if we want to be effective. And, in some cases, if we want to survive.

Sometimes we find ourselves in church leadership scenarios where everything we touch turns to gold. Everything we know about church ministry and everything our peers are trying on for size dovetails perfectly in our context. But then our church grows, decreases in size, or is dealt a big morale blow, or we move on to another church, and all we have done in the past is no longer effective. The quirky leader draws from and recasts his or her plumblines in new landscapes.

One of the greatest bands of all time (whether you like their music or not), based simply on their ability to be relevant in any landscape, is the group U2. As of the writing of this paragraph, U2 holds the record for the highest grossing concert tour of all time, with an average of more than 66,000 people in attendance at every show. The band with the second-highest record is the Rolling Stones, with an average of more than 32,000 at each show. The Rolling Stones are certainly another band that has stood the test of time.

Both U2 and the Rolling Stones, while very different in musical style, are often described as bands that create *timeless music*. Both bands were considered relevant in every decade they've existed. Their frontmen, Bono and Mick Jagger respectively, are two of the most recognizable faces in pop culture.

And, for the time being, they still have our attention. Bono is a force to be reckoned with as a humanitarian and activist to the degree that his reputation as an influencer stands independent of U2. Mick Jagger is not a humanitarian, activist, politician, or anything of the sort, but he has still managed to reinvent himself in ways that make him one of the most influential frontmen in history and the embodiment of self-expression and counter-culture for young and old. Mick has a perfect combination of confident attitude and humility, with an ability to adapt his quirkiness to different situations. This is why the sixty-nine-year-old made a perfect host for the finale of *Saturday Night Live's* 2012 season, where he played roles in comedy sketches that lampooned himself.

If rock stars read the signs, pay attention, and adapt to their audience, how much more so should we as church leaders? We have to be ongoing students of our particular landscapes and the new landscapes we find ourselves in so we don't become one hit wonders, academics with one-size-fits-all solutions, or the stand-up comedians who are a joke to a changing audience. Mark Twain said, "Give a man a reputation as an early riser and he can sleep 'til noon." May it never be.

THE PROBLEM WITH LAKE HOUSES

One of our favorite family movies is *Dan in Real Life*. In short, the story is about an advice column writer who has dreams of syndication while living in the wake of his wife's death, discerning and responding to problems of budding romances with his teenage daughter, and dealing with the more than slightly problematic problem of falling in love with his brother's girlfriend.

I won't completely spoil the plot for you. You need to see it if you haven't. Or see it again if you have. But I will point out one little observation. I'm assuming the writers/director/producer knew exactly what they were doing with *setting* in this story. I assume that to draw attention to Dan's *real-life* problems, they place him in an ideal, perfect, *far from real-life* setting. If the unrealistic setting wasn't purposeful, it's a welcome irony.

The entire movie takes place at Dan's parents' lake house during an annual family gathering. At the lake house, mom rises early and makes breakfast. The house is tidy. The landscaping is immaculate. Mom and dad don't raise their voices at one another. The bedrooms are perfectly maintained, as they have always been. Everyone looks forward to family game time, where the competition is friendly. Family skit night allows everyone to express him or herself, laugh together, and celebrate each other's quirks. Everyone looks out for the other. At one point, multiple young children go missing for hours, and no one calls the police. In this lake house world, bad things are an obvious anomaly. Dan's problems are the only *real* problems in this *real* life.

This setting doesn't exist in real life. It surfaces our own need to face our real-life problems against a backdrop that is predictable, fairy tale, and full of forced sentimentality. The problem of the movie for me is not Dan having to come to grips with the fact that even advice columnists don't have all the answers; it's that we have to come to grips with the fact that our own ideal world does not exist.

I wonder how many moms watch this movie and cry over the fact that their children don't talk to one another. Or that they are losing their homes. Or that their husbands are not as sensitive and understanding and wise as John Mahoney's character. I wonder how many men (the ones who analyze chick flicks) watch this movie and dream of their wives being the perfect woman who is well read, independent yet in desperate need of a man to settle and comfort her, who exercises every day in sexy outfits like Juliette Binoche's character.

I wonder how many church leaders believe there exists a setting in which everyone is on board with the mission, the staff never disagrees, everyone's motives are pure, sin is confessed without struggle or confrontation, everyone gets to be creative in his or her own way without divergence, and people instinctively flock to the waters of baptism.

There is no real life like this real life.

This is great news for the quirky leader! Life does not fit into a pretty package. There are no straight lines. There are no perfect scenarios. Even church life is screwed up and awkward. Yes! We belong!

It's A Two-Way Mirror

Everyone in your church has an ideal church in his or her own mind, with an ideal leader. In many cases, the picture looks a lot like a lake house gathering and lifestyle.

The quirky leader can do two things in response to this vision of churchtopia:

1. Let them see you sweat.

2. Take them behind the façade.

Old-school conventional wisdom says leaders should be the shoulder to cry on instead of the ones crying. They should be the rock. They are fearless and point the way with unshakable confidence.

The problem with this leadership mindset is that no one ever feels that way in real life. If we fake it 'til we make it and people don't see through the fallacy, we set ourselves up to be rock star leaders with no more than roadie credibility when the fit hits the shan. We run the risk of great failure in our own mind and in the mind of everyone else we allowed to keep us on our pedestal of perfection.

A lot of people in your church want you to be a rock star. Because they want to be one. Because they were sold a lie that they *can* be one.

In their minds, the only sweat that comes from a rock star is the sweat that comes from performing brilliantly and passionately for the crowd that lives vicariously through them.

They want you to be real, but not *too* real. They want rock stars on a leash.

They want you just poor enough to be humble and far from *worldly*. They want you just smart enough to be wise but far from cocky. Just sinful enough to know the thrill of redemption but not enough to be labeled experienced. Just cool enough to be attractive to their friends but not so cool that you love your own reflection in the mirror.

Unfortunately, we tip the scales in all those areas from time to time, and if the people we lead don't think we have the ability to fall, the drop will be long and lonely on the way down.

Let them see you sweat. Help them navigate real life.

Foster relationships with them so they get to see past your exterior. While it can be painful at times to realize your rock stars fight similar battles, it's often refreshing to know their songs come from a place of real experience, real hurt, real frustration, and real disillusionment, and those situations are met with real hope. Hope can be recognized as real only against the backdrop of real adversity.

I sometimes can't stomach music from some corners of the Christian subculture for this very reason. It's not believable. It's hard to trust the message of hope from a pre-pubescent girl who just went through Christian music's equivalent of Disney's pop idol sweetheart machine. It's suspect at best.

Speaking of Disney, have you ever done the back-lot tour? I did as a kid. I wish I hadn't. It was messy. I saw broken animatronics. Discarded costumes. With Disney, it's probably better to believe magic is real, streets are always tidy, and nothing ever breaks down. We need to vacation in those spots where life is perfect for a bit. The back-lot tour crushed my pretend world. They don't do themselves any favors by showing people their back lot.

You don't do yourself favors by not giving tours of yours.

Invite them to your house, and let them see your socks on the floor. Let them see your kids fight. Let them hear about your fears and failures and deepest prayers. Let them know what you've come through.

Don't be the cocky self-made lawyer on the television show *Suits* who said, "Sometimes I like to hang out with people who aren't that bright, you know, just to see how the other half lives." You aren't that cool. Deep down, you know that.

I started this chapter with the idea that leadership life experience counts. But it only counts for 50 percent or less. *Sharing* that experience pays dividends. Embrace your past, envision the future in light of it, gain perspective, elevate Jesus, pay your lessons forward, tear down the façades, remember what's worth fighting for. Enlighten others with that story.

CHAPTER EIGHT:
UNIQUE, UNPREDICTABLE, AND MEMORABLE

I'm grateful that they showed the way 'cause I could
never know the way to serve Him on my own. I want to
be a clone.

From the song "I Want to Be a Clone"
by Steve Taylor

Everyone has quirks. They make us interesting and give us a platform. Hiding our quirks makes us boring and ineffective. No one wants to be part of a Stepford Church where everyone looks and talks the same way. Right?

When we start to celebrate our quirks, the world takes notice. The world wants to get to know us better. When we begin to talk about the things that make us unique, the world asks questions. When we celebrate our unique point of view, we invite the world into dialogue with us. Celebrating your own leadership quirks inspires others to do the same.

Leaders who celebrate their own quirks become Pied Pipers for people who have been in hiding, because they instill a sense of freedom in them to bring what they offer to the table. There is nothing more encouraging to a leader who thinks a little left of center than to see another leader taking risks and paving new roads.

I hope no one picked up this book and stopped reading in Chapter 2 somewhere. While I firmly believe everything we've covered about stepping up and being a strong champion of vision, not apologizing for your quirks, feeling good about saying "no" from time to time, being right, protecting your church's character, and so on, and I believe I gave plenty of parenthetical asides to make room for deviation, I fear something will get lost in translation.

Part of our jobs as quirky leaders is certainly about finding and celebrating our own voice while yielding and listening to the Spirit in our own unique setting. But it doesn't stop there. The quirky leader has to understand he or she has a whole church full of quirky people.

Those people are also there for a reason. They aren't just there for us to carve out our own version of churchtopia. They are there because they have something unique to say. If this sounds counter to anything you understood me to say earlier, please let me explain further.

Protecting the vision is vital. Protecting it is sometimes a matter of subjective taste. The leader cannot apologize for that. At the same time, the quirky leader must innovate alongside other quirky people. Help them find their place. Help them find their voice. Teach them to read the signs as well.

At times, a leader will have to say no. This is standard in any organization with a mission, vision, and values. This is standard when it comes to protecting brand. Leaders cannot be burdened with an expectation to say yes to every unique and crazy idea that comes to their attention.

Saying yes to unique and crazy people is something altogether different. Or, if you prefer, let's call them the church. The bride. The Imago Dei.

MODELING FREEDOM AND GIVING PERMISSION

The first time I remember experiencing freedom to lead was in high school. My speech teacher encouraged me to apply for a position at a local radio station to do the sports updates for our school. I loved the idea of radio, but I hated sports. "What's more important to you?" he asked me. "The opportunity, or ironing out the specifics about what you *think* they are going to expect?" The opportunity sounded incredible, but I didn't know what he meant about "what I *thought* they were going to expect."

"Obviously, they expect me to report on sports," I told him.

"What does that look like?" he asked. I proceeded to tell him about all the boring sports announcers I knew of.

"Well, I guess you got it all figured out then," he said.

Confused still, but knowing he was trying to teach me a lesson, I applied for the job. In the interview, they asked me about my personality and how that would come across over the radio. I told them that some people would probably describe me as a class clown, a little irreverent at times, and someone who was fun to be with. That's how my girlfriend described me, anyway (who later said "yes" to marrying me). That all sounded great to them. They hired me that day and said my first show would happen the following week.

We had a studio at the school where they said we could record the program and deliver a, ahem, *cassette tape* to the station. My teacher was at the first taping. I started to record the sports update with him and my friend in the room. As I talked, it felt awkward. My teacher spoke up and said, "This doesn't sound like you at all."

My friend and I started joking around and putting on our *radio voices*. We pretended we were reporting from an undisclosed offsite location. "That's more like it," my teacher said.

"What? You think they're going to buy a comedy routine at the station?" I chortled. "They hired me to do the news."

"Yes. Indeed. They hired *you* to do the news. Give them *you*. Trust me. They'll want to listen to the show. The sponsors will be happy. The audience will appreciate it much more than a couple of high school kids trying to be something they aren't. And you'll probably have quite a few fans around the school who tune into a radio station they never listen to in order to hear the show."

The next day, I delivered a tape of "The Rob and Jay Show" (for some reason, we felt we needed aliases) to the station. They loved it. They appreciated our taking liberties and having fun. We did shows "all over the world" (from the studio or my living room). People loved it.

The one temporary disappointment came from one of our sponsors. He hated it. He wanted his sports update to the point with no tomfoolery. I remember the look of anger on his face as he stormed into the radio station and threatened to pull his sponsorship. I remember the conversation in which the station told him he was free to do whatever he wanted, but as far as they could tell, our show had way more listeners than they ever expected, and his name was attached to our success. There were other sponsors willing to step up and be connected to the show.

He stayed on as a sponsor, but he wasn't thrilled. He told us he thought we were embarrassing ourselves and we were going to get a big wake-up in the real world one day. "Grow up," he said.

My speech teacher laughed when he heard that. "That's because he's content to never change. It's that attitude that will make it hard for him to stay in business a long time."

He was right. Last I heard, a kid from my high school bought the man's struggling business, updated and expanded it, and is quite successful. But that's beside the point (or is it?).

Later that year, I was asked to emcee ceremonies at the school on numerous occasions, including a regular gig in our school assemblies. I started to take risks in other classes with the way I did assignments, such as reciting my memorized portion of *Beowulf* in a British accent in my English class or bringing an amp and guitar to debate class for my opening remarks.

The more I think about this speech teacher, the more I am certain I need to write him a thank you letter. He would often teach his classes outside or offsite. He encouraged us to start new clubs around the school, let us out of class early if we could prove there was a good reason to do so, signed recommendation letters for us, changed the direction of the desks in the classroom just for the sake of change and to keep us guessing, allowed us to listen to music while studying, and used every bit of multimedia he had available to him at the time to frame lessons and get us thinking. He gave me the first lesson in asking, "Who said you can't do that?" He gave permission and modeled freedom.

I could replace every character and situation from my high school experience with numerous people and stories from church experiences over the years. There are always situations in which we think we know what everyone expects. There is always a bit of risk when we test those waters or throw someone a curve ball. There is always a small business owner who is proud of his conventional ways. There is always fear of upsetting that business owner because he  funds the project in part and feels like he can throw his weight around because of it. There are too many small business owners closing shop because they are too proud to change or admit they were wrong.

I'm thankful for the many, many teachers in my life who are not afraid to inspire individuals to be themselves for the sake of something greater than what they would have been if they had settled for being someone they aren't.

UNIQUE AND YOU-NIQUE

The Bible is full of quirky people. Some had forts in the woods where people would go to hear them talk, some dressed funny, some danced naked, some burned poo and made bread over it. Today, we celebrate these weirdoes because they made a difference. Their uniqueness gave them a unique mission field. It is the same for us today.

God has made each person unique in order for that person to discover his or her own mission field. I cannot reach the people God has called you to reach. I'm uniquely shaped to reach a group of people you can't. This is true on a personal level and an organizational level. Your church can reach the people in your town in ways I couldn't imagine and vice versa. If Jesus' last command (go and make disciples) is our greatest concern, it is imperative we do some self-discovery and identify our unique voice(s) in the world. If we conceal our quirks and toe the line, the world is robbed of missionaries.

Two obvious things make us unique: our story and the place we live. We know when we tell our story it will resonate with someone at some time. Maybe not everyone. But someone. So we keep telling. We know the place we live has special traits and oddities we need to pay attention to and speak into. Obviously, you know your town way better than I do and are uniquely privileged to speak into its idiosyncrasies and take advantage of its opportunities.

But we rarely talk about our own personal quirks in the same light. Maybe someone told us they aren't welcome. Maybe we don't know how to channel them. Maybe we are afraid. Maybe we spend our time trying to bend them or morph them into something else—the thing we think people want.

Betty lives with Jesus now, but she used to go to my church growing up. Man, she was . . . different. She had crazy hair like Doc in the *Back to the Future* movies. She had a mustache. She wore the same dress a lot. She grunted. But man, she loved Jesus. She showed that love for him by doing the best thing she knew how to do. She prayed.

Her gifts weren't spectacular by any stretch of the imagination, but she prayed. More than you and I put together. She would walk neighborhoods and pray. She would ask waitresses in restaurants if she could pray for them.

Some would never dream of striking up a conversation with Betty if they passed her on the street. She was odd. But as she passed by, she would pray for them. As such, many people ended up coming to the church, because they wondered why someone like Betty loved them so much.

Betty didn't have a burn-on to lead any prayer ministry in the church. She didn't feel it was her place. But I've met a few Bettys since then who do have some interesting prayer ideas. They aren't all bad ideas, but some ideas have a lot of misfired synapses and unconnected dots.

Donna (who is also with Jesus) once told me God gave her a clear vision of me laying hands on every person at the end of each service every week and praying for them. She was what some call a "prayer warrior." Honestly, I learned a lot from her. She was dedicated. She met with teams every week and prayed for me and others during the service on Sunday. She believed deep in her being that this new direction was the route to go, and while she didn't say it exactly like this, she believed for me to say "no" would be disobedience to the Spirit.

She was wrong. My immediate thought was, "Why did God give you the message and keep it a secret from me?" It certainly was an odd conviction. But to write her off as crazy would have been not to go the distance. Simply to challenge her would have been missing out on an opportunity to examine other ways prayer might have a focus in our church.

So we set off on a journey. She told me all her prayer stories. I told her mine. She told me about all the times she had seen prayer change things in dramatic ways. I told her some of the same and added stories about the times where prayer went weird and people made me feel guilty about not praying *their way*. The stories led to us sharing the labels people put on us. Some flattering. Some painful. She told me why she carried the mantel, and I shared why I'm sometimes cautious. The end result was a mutual understanding that led to many fruitful prayer experiences in our church with Donna at the helm.

Will is a fire-breather. Really. His whole appearance is a snapshot of a quintessential circus sideshow performer—all the right tats and all the right piercings. He's relatively new to Jesus. We love him. I love him. One day he Facebooked me and said, "I breathe fire. Is there a place for me?" The answer is yes. He ended up breathing fire for us at an outdoor gathering last year to welcome newcomers to the church. Since then, Will has taken on a few jobs at parties for people in the church and made even more contacts through those.

Now, to be fair, in a lot of church contexts Will might have a hard time putting that skill to work for the kingdom. But what's sad is that in many churches there wouldn't even be a conversation to dig deeper and see what makes Will tick.

The church could have worked hard to fit Will's fire-breathing in and come up short with ideas. That doesn't let us off the hook. Fire-breathing isn't the only thing that makes Will unique. Beneath the fire-breathing is a man who is excited about starting a journey with Jesus and is looking for opportunities to speak into the culture that has embraced him *outside* the church—people who are disenfranchised and burnt by religion. Is Will different? You bet. So am I. So are you. So are Will's unique friends who might not relate to either of us. But because he is here, they are starting to come as well.

WHO WILL ASK THEM IN?

Janice auditioned for her music team at church. The band was usually composed of drums, guitar, bass, keys, and vocals—your standard rock band. But Janice showed up with a recorder. The kind you learned to play in first grade.

The folks running the audition hoped she didn't see the look on their faces as she pulled it from its case. When she said she wanted an audition, she mentioned voice, but not this. She began to play what she said was the song "As the Deer." But that deer was not panting for water. It was screaming in agony. It was awful.

Tearful, Janice put it down. She knew she had done a bad job. She asked if she might go over to the piano and play a song instead. They obliged, but strike two.

Finally, Janice asked if she could sing. "Absolutely," said the music pastor. She began to sing for the people auditioning her. It was not a good end to the audition. Her voice was equally as bad as her instrumental endeavors.

She thanked the team and asked them to forgive her. "I shouldn't have come today. I knew it was a risk."

But the pastor asked if she could stay a little longer. They went into another room, and he asked her why she wanted to be

part of the band. "It always looks like you guys are having fun. Like you enjoy what you do. I want to be able to enjoy serving too."

The pastor asked, "Do you enjoy playing music?"

"Not really; I'm not particularly good. As you already know. It's kind of a struggle for me."

She went on to describe the business she ran. She cleaned homes for people and house-sat for them when they were on vacation. She took care of their pets and gardens and sometimes even fixed things around their home. "It's the only time I feel like I'm worth something. When I take care of other people's things for them."

Janice now leads the hospitality team at her church. She developed the coffee ministry. She organizes the cleaning teams. She makes breakfast for the band and runs a team of people who do likewise. She also makes herself available to take care of people's homes for free when they can't afford to do it on their own. She started by getting groceries for her neighbor who is confined to a wheelchair.

This is possible because the church created a budget line to hire her when there is a need to fill.

She still can't play recorder. No one cares. Including her.

In some settings, Janice would have been allowed to play recorder or piano or sing simply on the merits of her heart. This would have been a tragedy. Pity placement would have been painful for everyone who had to listen to her for sure, but even more importantly, it would have done her a disservice as her true voice continued to lie dormant.

In many settings, Janice would have gone back to hiding away, or she would have eventually moved on. Crushed. Feeling unwanted. It took someone asking some simple questions to get Janice on a path of discovering her own voice.

CHANGE FOR THE SAKE OF CHANGE

I am writing in a coffee shop a couple of hours from home. I needed a change of pace and atmosphere. I needed new inspiration. I find if I sit at my desk in my office, no matter how much I love my surroundings and have made them uniquely mine (which sometimes means my desk is messy), I need fresh physical landscapes to inspire me. I need to order my coffee from a shop I don't go to all the time. I need to eat lunch in a restaurant I've never been to. I'm allergic to predictability. Most of the time.

I want some consistency for sure. I want to come home to my clean, comfortable home at night and sit in my most comfy chair. Maybe sip a scotch or enjoy an artisan cheese. I want consistency in my church where it helps people get assimilated into the life of the church.

But if you come into Westwinds and expect it to look the same week after week, you will be sorely disappointed. I don't think anyone is, though. People have come to expect the unexpected in our aesthetic.

Coriolis made a decision long ago that *changing for the sake of change* is not only acceptable in our environment but preferred. Changing some things up *just because* helps create a *setting* that does not get *set* in its ways.

JOIN THE ONGOING CONVERSATION AT QUIRKYLEADERSHIP.COM

This is obvious not only in our aesthetic choices but also in the flavor of programs and initiatives. Outward changes have become a working metaphor for us to talk through inward spiritual seasons and process life change with our people.

We try some fun things. They don't always work. In one particular instance, we took out every chair in the auditorium and created a tent-like atmosphere with pillows all over the floor. We invited people to kick off their shoes and join us on the floor in the round. All of our young people loved it! But we forgot to address the needs of people who had physical restraints and conditions that wouldn't allow them to participate. In a mad scramble to save face, our ushers pulled out a stack of chairs and scattered them around. We barely pulled that one off.

More often than not, however, our church loves the aesthetic changes. We love inspiring outside of our immediate context and have come to understand that influence as part of our role. We understand not all churches have the freedoms we do to change their environment. It's not our goal to provide aesthetic blueprints for people in order for their churches to have more eye candy. Our goal is to inspire individual creativity and freedom.

An environment that expects change is open to fresh ideas of all shapes and sizes. The complaint meter that measures *the way we used to do things* barely registers and invites everyone to pay attention and enter into the conversation. Change surfaces a *need to know* in people.

Over time, it is human nature to become numb to detail, the more accustomed we become. Change adds new paint to the canvas and piques intrigue. In these times, the leader has everyone's attention and is able to speak into things with a fresh voice. An environment of change allows us all to embrace new ideas as new people make our church their home.

If your environment is not accustomed to change at all, the learning curve may be steep. It's in these situations where self-disclosure and feed-forward is especially important. Feedback loops from trusted *plants* in your congregation can be a good idea as well (people who give you the word on the street).

Whenever we have a change of monumental proportions coming, we spend a good deal of time with our elder team talking about all the potential fallout. We try to identify the potential questions and answers before they even surface. Our elders then begin conversations with people in the church to tell them change is coming. Those people often bring up questions we didn't anticipate. And, as the news leaks and questions are answered along the way, the bomb diffuses.

Creating an environment that is ripe for change is the sugar that makes even the most bitter medicine go down easier.

Last night I saw a concert in a garden pavilion with one of my favorite Americana artists, the Steel Wheels. While introducing the last song, Trent, the leader of the band, described their love of music from generations before them. "We love this music, and we want to protect it and pass it on," he said. "We do that by taking it and messing it up a bit with our own musical bents and sharing it with our children. What we want more than anything is for our children to take it and mess it up a bit for their children as well. That's how it will survive."

Trent articulated what I value about change. Change doesn't always devalue or deconstruct the past; it builds on it. Change doesn't necessarily say the past methodology sucked (which devalues the people who once thought it was a good idea and invested themselves in it). It says, "Here's a fresh perspective in light of how things are changing around us." When people understand that momentum and motive, they are more apt to entrust their leaders with the future.

QUIRKY ANARCHY

Leaders often fear words like *freedom*. We fear things getting out of control, insubordination, cockiness, people throwing their weight around, the weak getting trampled underfoot, loud voices, and misalignment. Be ye not afraid. We can celebrate quirkiness, individuality, freedom, permission, and change and still have parameters and processes in place for our *organizations*.

David and I try to model a process from dream state to fruition for every big project, endeavor, and direction change we own. It looks something like this:

- Dreaming/loose plans

- Recruiting/stirring interest

- Testing

- Revisions

- Launch

The first stage is exactly what it sounds like. We get an idea. Maybe over breakfast. Maybe because we're bored. Maybe something born out of deep emotion over something unrelated. Maybe as a response to tragedy. Maybe as a potential answer to a problem or felt need. We tease that idea out in our own heads and with each other.

When the idea feels right and it won't go away, we bring others into our process. People we like. People who might have similar bents. Before it is even detailed. And we ask for input. Kibitzing. Feedback.

We then write abstracts and first drafts. We draw pictures and collect data. We start asking others what they think. If it's potentially controversial or a big change, this is the time we would ask for elder input. And spouse input (although that may come in the first phase as well). We surface all the potential problems. We ask our trusted intelligence, "What's the word on the street? Is this a good time? How will this go down? Does anyone care as much as we do?"

Once we feel good about all these steps, we launch. We actually do something. And we do it big. With all the people we brought into the process.

We want our staff and our people to follow suit. This process doesn't limit our freedom. It saves our butts. It keeps us on track. It includes others in the process. It invites the Spirit to speak from A to Z. When our staff and our people operate this way, they feel energized. Supported. Green-flagged. Effective. Useful. Innovative. Imaginative. Like they have something to share worth sharing.

The end result? Unique, unpredictable, and memorable dreams beyond our wildest first imaginations come to fruition. With a rag-tag bunch of freaks and geeks we call our church. Together. Shadowing God, building the church, and healing the world.

CHAPTER NINE:
DÉNOUEMENT

I took Shakespeare classes. Two semesters were dedicated to the playwright in my early college days. It seemed the thing to do. Other literature classes at the junior college were covering things I had already read in high school, and when I saw the people in the Shakespeare line at registration, they looked like my kind of people. One may have been wearing a cape.

Dénouement is a word I have heard only in Shakespeare classes. Most people would be fine with saying *the conclusion* or *the resolution*, but Shakespeare lovers are their own breed (our own breed?). And, quite frankly, the word describes something richer than *the end*.

The dénouement is the period of time between the end and where the end really begins. It's the *falling action*. It's the release of anxiety. It's the part of the story in which things start feeling right and normal, or at least the mysteries come to light. In Shakespeare's comedies, the protagonist enjoys a happy conclusion to the dénouement. In a Shakespearean tragedy, the dénouement is one in which the protagonist is in a worse place than he or she was at the beginning, and a lot of people usually die.

Dénouement is French. It comes from the French word *desnouer*, which means "to untie," and ultimately derives from the Latin word "nodus," which means "knot." The untying of the knot. Dénouement is also often described in terms of a *catharsis.* Catharsis comes from a Greek word meaning *purging* or *cleansing.*

My prayer at the onset of writing this book was and still is for you (the reader) to begin to untie the knot. Or, better yet, to end the cycle of being all tied up in knots. To be purged of the things that keep us in leadership-expectation prison and make us unfruitful, tired, misaligned, and depressed, with no sense of our true identity in Jesus.

I pray that as you read these final words, the dénouement of the book feels like a new beginning for you. While it is unrealistic to believe any of us will have the kind of silly endings that some Shakespearean comedies have, where people all get well, lovers end up together, evil is averted or eliminated, and everyone dances, no one wants to live in a tragedy. God is in the business of healing. It's not only A or B. There has to be a C.

I want us all to lead our churches with a spirit of freedom in Jesus that energizes us to do bold and beautiful things for the kingdom. I want it for you. I want it for me.

WARNING

Early on in the book, I talked about the privilege of being right in your context. While I believe everything I said, I fear some will use those words to fuel their own entitlement or give themselves license to be jerks.

While being *right* can often mean saying "No," I don't want you to get the idea that I somehow relish being a killjoy or the hoop everyone has to jump through. Sometimes, I am that guy. Sometimes, you will be that person. But being right looks more like daring to be different, going against the grain, taking risks, forging new territory, breaking down walls, and experiencing things beyond your wildest imaginations.

Of course, as exciting as that all sounds, we are human and sometimes think our prophetic doo doo doesn't stink.

This summer, I attended the Bonnaroo Music and Arts Festival with my son. It was our third trip to the 'Roo. Thousands of music and art enthusiasts travel to Manchester, Tennessee, year after year to participate in the monumental festival. While there is a prevalent message of *freedom* and *individuality* at this festival and similar festivals, everyone knows what it looks like when those things get out of hand. When there are no laws, no boundaries, and no precautions, *freedom* and *individuality* quickly turn into *stupidity* and *people getting hurt*.

There are signs around Bonnaroo that say "Don't be THAT guy." Everyone who attends knows who *that guy* is. He's the one who thinks he can't fail. He cuts in line. He drinks too much alcohol and bakes in the dehydrating sun and vomits on his friend's sleeping bag in their tent. He yells obnoxious mantras during your favorite band's show. He thinks he is above it all. He doesn't listen to his friend's advice.

Don't be leadership's equivalent of that guy.

In 1911, a guy named Bobby Leach took a barrel ride over Niagara Falls. He broke his jaw and his kneecaps. But he lived to tell his remarkable story.

People talked about him far and wide. He went on publicity tours for the rest of his life, telling his story and performing other daredevil stunts. It seemed like Bobby could get away with anything.

Until one day when he accidentally slipped on an orange peel. He broke his leg, got gangrene, had his leg amputated, and died from complications of the surgery.

Every leader, regardless of how amazing his or her story is and in spite of how different and unique and daring and *awe-inspiring* he or she might be, is one orange peel and one bit of carelessness away from devastation.

Don't be a leadership Leach. Leak Jesus.

In early talks with my publisher, the people who are responsible for printing and distributing this book you're holding, we talked about the "branding" of authors. Some guys are known as the "smart" authors. Some ladies are known as the "spiritual insight" authors. Someone along the line suggested I think of myself as the "envelope pusher" author.

That didn't sit well with me.

I don't want to be that guy (necessarily). At least, not in the ways I immediately thought of that guy. I want to be a guy who stands "for" something rather than the guy who always stands "against." If I'm holding up a proverbial sign at the side of the road, I don't want it to condemn. I want it to give freedom.

"Envelope pusher" isn't completely wrong for the role I sometimes play as a leader, but I'd rather be known as the "Who said you can't do that?" guy. I want to be a leader who asks questions about the status quo and challenges conventional wisdom that has dried up and gone sour. I think God wants that for you too.

Not "prodding and poking." But rather, "engaging and shifting."

Not "yelling and screaming." But rather, "crying and pleading."

Not "piss and vinegar." But rather, "life and energy."

Not "deconstructing and devaluing." As much as, "evaluating and inventing."

As a leader in the church, I sometimes get angry. I'd like to think it's a righteous anger. A holy discontent. But I want to be motivated by love.

I want my impact and influence to be marked by Jesus. At Westwinds, we are fond of saying we want to live life with people so they can't help but rub up against us and get some Jesus on them.

Don't you want that? For yourself? For your church? For your community? For the kingdom?

Dénouement

You haven't been given permission just to make the tough calls; you've been given permission to be a voice in your community. You've been given permission to meet the needs of your city better than anyone else has or can. You've been given permission to dream up things that the "religious" community would never approve of. You've been given permission to piss off the powers of darkness.

Quirky Leadership Exercises

The Blind LEGO the Blind

Tools needed: Multiple LEGO projects (less than 50 pieces in a box).

Break into teams (4 people is a good team). Appoint one person as the leader on each team. Each leader is handed the instructions and picture for the final LEGO product. Each leader must describe to their team how to assemble the project without actually touching any of the pieces and without telling them what it should become in the end. Time limit 10-15 minutes.

Objective: At end of activity, ask the team to talk about the process. What was frustrating? What was fun? You'll probably hear things like, "Leadership is hard. Leadership requires reciprocal trust. Leadership matters. Creative collaboration can be difficult. Everyone needs to know his or her role. There can only be one vision."

Playdoh Your Strengths

Tools needed: Multiple cans of Playdoh or clay. A place to get messy.

Cover tables with paper or get your team around a surface that can get dirty. Ask everyone to create a sculpture that is a metaphor for what you imagine your organization can be.

Objective: First time we did this exercise the laughter in the process was worth the time spent. However, you can also learn a lot about the hopes and dreams of your people and surface the things they believe they are good at. This is a good way to affirm them, give them permission, challenge them to stretch, celebrate what they have done, and dream about the future. A related exercise might be to also have your team create a clay metaphor they believe represents the current state of the organization. Of course, this can be risky so, be ready for potentially uncomfortable conversation if someone decides to get real honest and work out what they've been feeling through a clay sculpture.

Post-it Parade

Tools needed: Multiple colors of Post-it pads.

Invite your team to walk around your church building (offices, auditorium, bathrooms, kid's space . . . everywhere) and place a post-it note anywhere that area surfaces a quirk in them.

Objective: Learn about others' quirks but also surface your own quirks in the process. Be prepared for your team to point out things you've never noticed. You might be surprised how long it's been since you've taken a stroll through your entire building.